flirting
sam van rood

For over 60 years, more than 50 million people have learnt over 750 subjects the **teach yourself** way, with impressive results.

be where you want to be
with **teach yourself**

For UK order enquiries: please contact Bookpoint Ltd, 130 Milton Park, Abingdon, Oxon, OX14 4SB. Telephone: +44 (0) 1235 827720. Fax: +44 (0) 1235 400454. Lines are open 09.00–17.00, Monday to Saturday, with a 24-hour message answering service. Details about our titles and how to order are available at www.teachyourself.co.uk

For USA order enquiries: please contact McGraw-Hill Customer Services, PO Box 545, Blacklick, OH 43004-0545, USA. Telephone: 1-800-722-4726. Fax: 1-614-755-5645.

For Canada order enquiries: please contact McGraw-Hill Ryerson Ltd, 300 Water St, Whitby, Ontario, L1N 9B6, Canada. Telephone: 905 430 5000. Fax: 905 430 5020.

Long renowned as the authoritative source for self-guided learning – with more than 50 million copies sold worldwide – the **teach yourself** series includes over 500 titles in the fields of languages, crafts, hobbies, business, computing and education.

British Library Cataloguing in Publication Data: a catalogue record for this title is available from the British Library.

Library of Congress Catalog Card Number: on file.

First published in UK 2006 by Hodder Education, 338 Euston Road, London, NW1 3BH.

First published in US 2006 by The McGraw-Hill Companies, Inc.

The **teach yourself** name is a registered trade mark of Hodder Headline.

Copyright © 2006 Sam van Rood

Typeset by Transet Limited, Coventry, England.
Printed in Great Britain for Hodder Education, a division of Hodder Headline, 338 Euston Road, London, NW1 3BH, by Cox & Wyman Ltd, Reading, Berkshire.

The publisher has used its best endeavours to ensure that the URLs for external websites referred to in this book are correct and active at the time of going to press. However, the publisher and the author have no responsibility for the websites and can make no guarantee that a site will remain live or that the content will remain relevant, decent or appropriate.

Hodder Headline's policy is to use papers that are natural, renewable and recyclable products and made from wood grown in sustainable forests. The logging and manufacturing processes are expected to conform to the environmental regulations of the country of origin.

Impression number   10 9 8 7 6 5 4 3 2 1
Year   2010 2009 2008 2007 2006

contents

acknowledgements

Firstly and most importantly I would like to thank all of my clients, who have trusted me with their stories, hearts and most intimate dating secrets and who pay me to do what I love.

Thanks to the team at Hodder. Victoria for her harsh but fair editing and for coming up with the idea of **teach yourself flirting,** Jenny for putting up with my slight deadline lapses, Louisa in anticipation of some great marketing and everyone else who I didn't meet but made this book happen.

Thanks to my partners. Paul and James at Single Solution for a never ending supply of London singles, Lorraine at Gorgeous for my first ever big PR push and Martin and Marcus at Makefriendsonline for my first online agony uncle column and dating doctor surgery. Also thanks to Alexis, my first real client and the brain who got me started on the flirting path. Thanks also to the many journalists and people in the media who have found what I do interesting enough to write about, amongst their tough deadlines and tight schedules.

A big thanks has to go to Tracey Cox, whose work provides the foundation for my material and who is always up with the latest research. Also to Lowri Turner for her advice, guidance, friendship and sushi. Thanks to Warren Day, the Anthony Robbins trainer who has generously given so much of his time and taught me many of my most invaluable NLP (Neuro–Linguistic Programming) tools. Thanks to Paul McKenna, for his training and inspiring my mind programming CDs, and to Joseph O'Conner, whose brilliant book on NLP finally gave me the tools I had been seeking for so many years. And a big thanks to Chris James for his generous licensing terms and brilliant music that adds so much.

Thanks to Briege McCloon, for deciding to interview me for How to Find a Husband despite a very nasty case of the flu and the rubbish photos on my website. Thanks to Susie for opening all those doors that I didn't realise were so close. And a very big thanks to Fiona Godlee for giving me all those contracts that kept me fed while I was finding my feet.

Finally thanks to anyone who has helped me out and given me a break along the way, it's all those little steps that got me to where I am today.

dedication

This book is dedicated to Jane, whose wonderful love makes almost anything seem possible. And to Peta and Stephen, who raised me to believe that I could, and should, pursue my dreams. Thank you.

01

introduction

In this chapter you will learn:
- about the psychology of flirting
- that flirting is a skill that can be learned
- how successful, happy people flirt.

What you will get out of this book

Welcome to *Teach Yourself Flirting*. This is a practical, down-to-earth guide that will give you both the theory and practice that you need to master the basics of the art of flirting. You will start with the psychology of flirting and you will learn how flirting is a skill – just like riding a bike or learning to drive – that anyone, given the right training, can master. You will see how successful and happy people flirt by using simple techniques like listening and making people feel important.

You will then take a tour of the major flirting 'illnesses' – the most common things that will hold your flirting skills back. Each illness has an explanation and practical steps that you can take to 'cure' any flirting issues you might have.

Next you will learn the basics of flirting: how to give the right flirting signals; and how to read them. From there, you will be taught how to take the next steps, including making the first move, opening lines for both sexes, taking it further and learning to read the signs when the person you are flirting with is interested in you. And, of course, you will learn about that crucial part of flirting – closing the deal.

Finally, you will cover the other issues that surround the basics of flirting: safe flirting, flirting at work, flirting online and when speed-dating, flirting if you are gay, flirting if you are a student, and flirting in your later years.

This is a practical guide that will take you through the theory and psychology of flirting, but above all will give you the actual steps you need to take to flirt in real life and give you the tools to hone and boost your flirting skills.

Psychology of flirting

According to Kate Fox of the Social Issues Research Centre in Oxford, England, flirting is an essential and universal part of human interaction (SIRC Guide to Flirting, *What social science can tell you about flirting and how to do it*, Kate Fox, SIRC, 1999). Anthropologists have found flirting in some form or another in all cultures and societies around the world.

Flirting is an essential part of survival. It allows us to make contact with and mate with the opposite sex. Without flirting, we wouldn't be able to have offspring and humans would become extinct as a species. Because of this, flirting is a basic instinct and part of human nature.

Some evolutionary psychologists claim that flirting is the foundation of civilization as we know it. They argue that our brain is a device that has evolved to attract and retain partners – it is the equivalent to a peacock's tail, becoming more and more complex and spectacular as we wage the war to pass on our genes. According to these psychologists, all of our achievements in mathematics, great literature, and science are a side-effect of our ability and instinct to flirt.

Like all social interaction, flirting is governed by an unwritten set of laws that tell us where, when and how we should flirt. Psychologists and scientists have been studying how men and women interact and flirt for many years. But you don't need to read all of the research – the essence of their findings is contained in this book, and it has been tried and tested and worked into exercises and principles that you can easily put into practice. This is the start of your flirting journey.

My flirting journey

I'm Australian. I didn't realize until I left my country what a strong culture we have. One of those cultural features is friendliness, or, to put it another way, flirting. This was something that I just took for granted. I have travelled all around the world, met hundreds of people and I have always found it really easy, enjoyable and fun. It seemed as natural as a fish swimming in the sea. Part of this is also my background; now I look back on it, my mother was a natural flirt. I remember from my teenage years my mother meeting travellers down at the local shop and then asking them back for lunch. They would hang around for hours, eat lunch and chew the fat before moving on. Whenever we went to the local market to buy food, my mother would chat to the shopkeepers. She often seemed to meet people in the street. When I was a kid, I didn't really think about it; most of the time, it actually embarrassed me. Looking back on it, I have always found Australian culture to be open, friendly and flirtatious.

When I arrived in London, I was in for a rude shock. I vividly remember my first trip on the tube (London's metro system). Fresh off the boat, I was excited, I had arrived in this big new city, pursuing a change of career, leaving behind everything that I had known in Australia and starting over again. Naturally, since it was something that I had always done, I leant over, looked at the person sitting next to me on the tube and said, 'Hi, how are you doing?' In the past, this had always been an easy and natural thing to do. Usually a conversation would just start, we would chat about travel and, more often than not, I would either end up making a friend or finding out some great information about the place I was visiting. Not this time. The poor London commuter looked at me like I was some sort of demented axe murderer. I wasn't particularly fazed at first. There must be something strange with this person. They are having a bad day. But this was repeated over and over again in London. It started to really beat me down. What was different here? That was really the start of my flirting journey. The skill that I had naturally used all my life was suddenly lost when faced with a hard-nosed London commuter on the tube. I had to start from scratch, relearn the rules and adjust them for the cold London climate.

Over time, I came to realize that flirting is partly about a state of mind. It is about being open to new people, having fun. It is about thinking that people are innocent until proven guilty. This is a typically Australian attitude. You meet someone new and you presume that they are okay. You will chat with them. If you like them, you'll invite them back to your place for a BBQ. Just like my mother did! Suddenly I was faced with a very different attitude. That you are guilty until proven innocent.

I realized that there was something different between me and the average Londoner. That difference is partly cultural, but also, to a large extent, it is about flirting. Flirting is not just about finding a date; it is a state of mind, an attitude and a way of interacting with people:

- Flirting is an attitude and state of mind.
- It is about being open and presuming people are innocent until proven guilty.
- Flirting varies from culture to culture.

What is interesting is that my first impression is backed up by research, polls and thousands of subsequent conversations. London is generally considered to be a place where flirting is hard to do. Because of that, you have to focus on the key skills and lessons of flirting, which can then be applied anywhere.

There seem to be two main issues at stake for singles not just in the UK, but voiced by my clients from all over the world. The first is that sometimes there is a piece of the jigsaw that is missing. People are suffering from some sort of flirting illness that is holding them back: rejectaphobia, desperitis, successitis. The other issue is that they don't have one or more of the essential skills of flirting. Somehow they have missed out. They feel that they either have a piece of the jigsaw missing or are suffering some sort of 'flirting illness'. Ultimately, however, people often just haven't learned the skill of flirting because it is not around them.

Let's use an analogy with driving. In some areas, there is no question about learning to drive. I was brought up on a vineyard in the Adelaide Hills in South Australia and driving was a skill that I automatically picked up. My dad used to let me drive our truck around the vineyard. My grandfather took me for driving lessons, and taught me some very bad habits that my subsequent driving instructors had to drill out of me. In the Adelaide Hills, if you wanted to get anywhere, you had to be able to drive or have someone drive you. Otherwise, it was a 45-minute wait for the bus, which finished running at 5p.m. Driving, like flirting, was something that we all learned as part of the surroundings.

In other areas, however, learning to drive is not a given. My girlfriend is a Londoner. She doesn't know how to drive, because she doesn't need to. She can catch the tube or a bus. For her to learn to drive she would need to take lessons, and then it would be stressful, and she hates the London traffic. She finds it far easier to walk down to the shops, or when necessary to take a cab. She doesn't know how to drive because for her, in London, learning to drive is a skill that is not essential, and, in terms of her lifestyle and needs, an unnecessary expense.

Flirting is the same. Some people pick it up naturally as a skill, as part of their culture. It appears to be something completely automatic, natural. Actually, just like driving, it is a skill to be learned. This book is really for all those people who would like to learn/touch up those skills.

Flirting is not just good for finding a partner, it has a whole range of other uses as well. People who are taught to flirt double their sales, move more quickly up the career ladder, double networking leads from presentations, and are generally more successful in their professional and personal lives. Students who flirt make more friends. Flirting opens doors. In summary:

- Flirting is a skill like learning to drive.
- Though it seems to come naturally to some people, flirting can be learned.
- Flirting is important for social interaction and for your career.

Flirting is a skill

Flirting, ultimately, is just like riding a bike, or learning to drive a car. It is a skill with a series of basic rules – and you have to adapt those rules to the environment you are in. In the forest, driving can be a bit wild and exciting; on the road, there are strict rules that you have to abide by. With flirting, there is flirting for love, and flirting in your professional life. Both are fundamentally the same, but have different rules that need to be understood and respected.

What is really interesting about learning to drive on the road is that there is a strict series of rules when you are in a car – and as you travel you come to discover that the rules are slightly different in every country. Obviously, some countries drive on the other side of the road, which changes many of the rules. In England, some of the traffic signals are different from those in Australia. You get an orange light before the light goes from red to green. In Australia it just goes straight from red to green. Similarly, there are cultural differences with flirting which you need to be aware of. For instance, there can be huge differences between the Americans and the British. What would be acceptable for an American, striking up a conversation with a stranger, is totally unacceptable elsewhere. The flirting signals given out by women are also different in different countries. That said, there is a core set of flirting rules that is the same throughout most cultures.

One part of the skill that you need to learn with flirting is the signals – which will be covered in more detail in Chapter 5. The following case studies illustrate the basic principles of signals.

Case study

Eric was a stereotypical computer man: No luck with women, yet he was a lovely guy. Worst of all he thought that no one was interested in him. He had almost never seen a woman show any interest.

I worked with Eric on the most basic flirting skill for a man – to spot a green light. That is, to spot when a woman gives you eye contact. We went out in Covent Garden in London. Very busy, full of people and tourists. Amazingly, by the end of the night, he had seen women show more interest in him in one night than in the previous three years!

'I was blind. Now I've learned how to see', Eric proclaimed dramatically. He was a fast learner. At a seminar he got three phone numbers from women who had flashed him the green light. Just like when driving on the road, or riding a bike, learning to spot and pay attention to traffic signals is crucial.

Case study

If you are a woman, learning the skill of giving flirting signals is also crucial. Amy and Nina were very friendly, open and able to meet new people. The problem was that they didn't know how to attract the right guys and how to keep away the ones they didn't want to talk to. Also, they didn't know how to move from 'friendly' to 'flirting'. This is a skill that can be learned. We spent a number of sessions getting them both comfortable with giving green light signals to guys they fancied and red lights to the ones they didn't. They went out to put their skills into practice. Their conclusion?

'Oh my god, it was like we were like giant magnets, the men were flocking.'

It was just a matter of learning the skill of turning their green light signals in the right direction.

In summary:

- Flirting is a skill that you need to learn – like all new skills it might seem scary at first.
- The more you practise the easier flirting becomes.
- Flirting, like driving, has rules. These rules vary in the context that you use them, for instance, flirting at work.
- Flirting rules vary from country to country.
- Flirting has basic signals – 'green lights' which indicate interest.
- You need to spot the green light signals.
- You need to be able to give green light signals to the people you fancy.
- You also need to keep an eye out for green light signals and decide if you want to return them!

Successful, happy people flirt

It's true. Successful, happy people flirt.

Successful people flirt

> **Case study**
>
> First, flirting can boost your success at work. Rose has been described by many people as the best boss they ever had. She is an amazing woman. She has a whole string of firsts under her belt. Her secret? She flirts with everyone she meets, in the professional sense of flirting.
>
> Whenever she speaks to a person, Rose gives them 200 per cent attention. She makes them feel like they are the most important person in the world. It doesn't matter if she disagrees with their opinion, because she listens so intensely, they feel listened to and valued.
>
> Rose's employees are extraordinarily motivated. They feel that she values them and so they work harder for her. They work much longer hours and push themselves harder than for previous bosses. As a boss Rose doesn't spend much time with her staff, but the time that she does spend with them has an enormous impact. Almost everyone who works with Rose speaks about her in glowing terms.
>
> Obviously there are many other factors at play here – Rose is a terribly intelligent, motivated and energetic person. Yet the key is that in every interaction she is making people feel good. When someone makes you feel good, you want to help them. By flirting with every person she meets, Rose is creating an army of people who feel good about her and who want to help her out with her career. It makes her happier, and it certainly makes her much more successful.
>
> Flirting gives you a certain kind of shine. Rose shines above everyone else. When people interact with her they want to contribute to her success – they remember her. Her employees work extra hard to contribute to her success.

Happy people flirt

Professor Mihaly Csikszenthimalyi, has spent the last 25 years studying flow, or what makes people happy in their everyday life. One of the key factors that he has identified is that we are hardwired to get happiness from interacting with other people. (Mihaly Csikszenthimalyi, *Flow: the classic work on how to achieve happiness*, Rider, 2002.) In fact, many civilizations of the past have gone to extraordinary lengths to make sure that members of their societies don't spend time by themselves. Why? Because they know that, as human beings, being around other people makes us happy.

In studying tens of thousands of people and the quality of their daily life again and again, it was found that people have their most positive moods when they are with friends. Teenagers, adults and married people are happiest when with friends. Even when retired, we are happier with friends than with our partners or family.

People who flirt, that is people who are open to meet new people, find it much easier to make new friends and maintain those friendships. Have you ever met one of those people who seems to make friends easily? They seem to be able to go to any new environment and make connections with new people and forge new friendships.

This really struck me at a singles event where I was giving flirting advice. For a change, it was decided that I would be at the door meeting and greeting every single person who came in, giving them their name badges for the night. This meant that effectively I got to flirt briefly with every single person who was coming to the party. Once they had been ticked off, I made sure I gave them great eye contact, made a cheeky comment about their user name, did some extra flirtation if they were particularly attractive, told them that I was the dating expert for the evening and sent them on their way. For me this felt fantastic, connecting with every single person as they came in the door, paying attention to them, being interested and introducing myself. The more people I flirted with, the better I felt, and the cheekier I got. Some people were interested in getting flirting advice, some people weren't – for me it didn't really matter.

When I thought about it afterwards, I realized that what was unusual about that night was that I had the opportunity to flirt with every single person. Once I got in the room, it all became incredibly easy. People came to me. Once they started their conversations they were more open and friendlier than usual. We had much more fun. Conversations seemed to flow more and to be more cheeky. Really it was the easiest, most fun night, where I was the most in demand that I can remember.

Contrast that to a previous night where I was feeling a little under the weather and not particularly flirtatious. I didn't get to introduce myself to everyone who came in the room. Basically, I spotted the people who I thought were interested in having a chat about flirting and I went and introduced myself. This was much more hard work. People weren't so open and friendly, they didn't seem to react as well. I left the evening thinking, phew, glad that's over.

Flirting on the night when I saw everyone at the door made me much happier, and much more successful in terms of results for my business. It can do the same for you.

In summary:

- Successful, happy people flirt.
- Business can be enhanced with a little flirting.
- Flirting makes other people feel good; it gives you a special 'shine' that marks you out from the crowd.
- Being around friends gives people their most positive moods.
- Flirting every day makes social interaction and making friends easier.
- Flirting smoothes the wheels of social interaction.

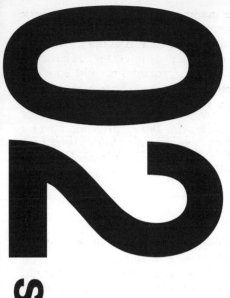

02

safe flirting

In this chapter you will learn:
- about safe flirting and getting flirting protection
- about controlling your drinking and date rape drugs
- that, fundamentally, flirting is safe.

Flirting has many benefits, but there are also some potential dangers that you need to be prepared for. Here are some easy, basic steps so that you can flirt with peace of mind.

Get flirting protection

This is something that I recommend to all my clients when they are starting in the dating world. Having flirting protection is a bit like having safe sex. By using a condom, you want to be able to have all the fun without any of the dangers. If you need to walk away, you need to be able to do it, quickly, easily and safely.

Flirting email address

Get a separate flirting email address. You can easily have a free web-based email address from services such as Yahoo and Hotmail. The idea of having a flirting email address is that you can hand out your email address without having to worry about it. If the person you are flirting with turns out to be an email stalker, you can get rid of your flirting email address and start again. Nothing lost. With a flirting email address, you can hand out your details with complete peace of mind.

Flirting mobile phone

It may be worth investing in a flirting mobile phone. These days, you can easily pick up a cheap pay-as-you-go mobile phone that you can just throw away if you need to. This means you can chat to the person over the phone and get to know them before you take things further.

This is particularly important for internet dating. You may get on well by email, but the next step in the filtering process is talking to them over the phone. Having a flirting mobile phone means they can call you, you can check them out, and if things don't work out you have nothing to worry about.

Having a flirting mobile phone is about having peace of mind. When you hand out your contact details, there is no need to worry that the other person is going to be calling you in the middle of an important business meeting, or in the middle of the night. You can turn off your flirting mobile phone or, if things get really bad, throw it away. All the benefits with none of the disadvantages.

One of my clients had some cards printed out specifically for dating. On the card, she had her dating email address and her dating mobile phone number. Perfect for speed-dating and other singles events.

Giving out personal details

If you have a flirting email address and mobile phone number, there is no reason to give out your actual personal details until you really get to know the person. You might want to wait at least until after three or four dates. By that time, you will really know if the other person is a serious prospect or not. At that point, you should feel safe and comfortable giving out your personal details.

Don't give money

You need to be aware that with the rise of internet dating websites, there has been a considerable rise in the number of people trying to commit fraud through websites. This is the classic honey trap, and it goes something like this:

1 You will be approached online by a very attractive woman, or indeed man, usually from an African, Russian or Eastern European country.

2 You will talk online, he/she will email you frequently, and soon start professing his/her love for you, or that he/she wants to come and visit you.

3 There will be some sort of emergency, where he/she doesn't have the money for the flight, and he/she will ask you for it.

4 The money will need to be sent by wire transfer.

5 If you send any money you will never see it or him/her ever again.

If anyone starts asking you for money when you are flirting online or in the real world, give them a wide berth.

Controlling your drinking

When you are flirting, it is important that you also control your drinking. Not only is excessive drinking bad for your health, it impairs your decision making. For the same reason that you shouldn't drink and drive, when you flirt you should stay sober. In both cases, you are making important decisions.

On first dates, the best rule is not to drink. Do something fun during the day, and get to know the person without alcohol getting in the way. At most, have one or two drinks.

Date rape drugs

You should be aware of date rape drugs when you are out flirting. This counts for both men and women.

Date rape drugs like Rohypnol and GHB are illegal in the UK and the USA, and there is much debate on how common they are. According to one article in *The Guardian* newspaper, one in four women reported that they had their drink spiked.

The difficulty with date rape drugs is that they are powerful: ten times stronger than valium. Victims are usually confused and completely lose their memory. All traces of the drugs are gone from your body within 12 hours. There are also some claims that 70 per cent of date rape drugs are administered by people known to the victim.

You should be aware of the dangers of date rape drugs and take basic precautions. Safety tips:

- Never accept a drink from a stranger.
- Always buy your drinks yourself.
- Make sure you tell your friends that if you seem to suddenly become very drunk, they *MUST* look after you and should *NEVER* allow you to go off with a stranger.
- The same counts for your friends. If they ever seem to suddenly become very drunk, you must look after them and get them out of the bar as soon as possible.

Really, it is pretty safe out there

With all this talk about safety, you have to remember that providing you use common sense it is pretty safe out there for flirting – take the attitude of innocent until proven guilty and put in place some basic safety precautions. In all my years of working with clients, I have never known anyone to have a serious problem with people through flirting.

In summary:

- Get a flirting email address, perhaps a flirting mobile phone and cards with your flirting contact details.
- Don't give out your real personal details until the fourth or fifth date.
- If someone asks for money, dump them quick.
- Control your drinking.
- Be aware of the dangers of date rape drugs.
- Remember, flirting is basically safe, but you need to take some precautions so that you can have the fun without the dangers.

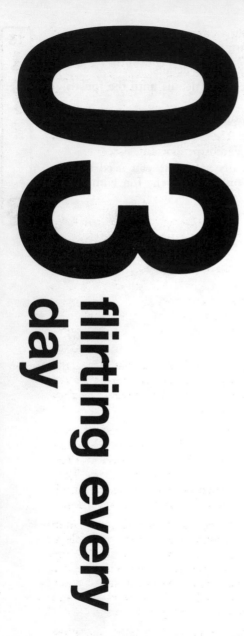

03

flirting every day

In this chapter you will learn:
- about listening skills
- how to flirt by making people feel important
- that people in relationships can flirt too.

Flirting is not just about finding a partner. Flirting is something that you can use every day – with your work colleagues, walking down the street, in the shops. People who flirt are more successful and they are happier. They seem to have a certain shine about them that allows them to glide through social interactions. People remember them. Things are easier for them. There is a couple of very simple things you can do to bring flirting into your life every day. The first and most important of these is terribly simple, but incredibly important: listening.

Listening

Listening is one of the most powerful flirting tools that you have in your arsenal. Yet often it is one of the most underused.

Essentially, people like people who listen to them. Or, rather, people like to talk, and like people to listen to them. It makes them feel important. It makes them look good. What is particularly strange is that if you spend an entire conversation listening to someone, they will usually remember the conversation as being terribly interesting, and they will think that you made some fantastic points.

Lots of books talk about the power of listening, but it is really important to experience this power. Most people think they are listening, but they don't realize the impact they have when they withdraw their attention from someone.

Words that people use when describing how they feel when a person is listening to them are all terribly positive. They feel listened to and important, they enjoy the conversation and feel very positive towards the person who is listening to them. They describe the experience as being much more focused, and find it much easier and more enjoyable to carry on the conversation.

Compare that with when a conversation is withdrawn. Often people use the terms 'arrogant', 'angry', 'infuriated', 'worthless' – one person actually said to me that they wanted to slap the person who wasn't listening to get their attention! Also, interestingly, people actually find it much harder to speak when someone isn't listening, they lose track of the conversation and their thoughts. The whole experience is very unpleasant.

This is the power of listening. Simply by paying complete attention to the person you are listening to, you will massively boost their impression of you and the positive associations that they have with you. This is fundamentally what flirting in everyday life is about – making the person that you are talking to feel good so that they enjoy the conversation and see you in a brighter light.

Exercise

Right now, remember a time when someone was not listening to you, or was pretending to listen. Maybe it was a work colleague or someone in a shop. Remember what this time looked, sounded and felt like. Now, below, write your thoughts about the person.

....

....

Right now, circle a number to indicate how positively you remember the person who wasn't listening, where 0 is totally negative and 10 is totally positive.

0   1   2   3   4   5   6   7   8   9   10

Right now, have a quick stretch, and remember a time when a person was listening to you totally intently, where they were really interested in what you were saying. Now write down your impressions of that person.

....

....

Right now, circle a number to indicate how positively you remember the person who was listening, where 0 is totally negative and 10 is totally positive.

0   1   2   3   4   5   6   7   8   9   10

Go back and contrast the two scores and the two impressions you had of the people. This is the power of listening. You have the same power to make either a good or bad impression based on how much you listen.

Exercise

Listening with a friend
Step 1

Sit down with a friend. Talk about a topic you normally would chat about. Listen as you would normally. Then ask them how comfortable they were talking to you on a scale of 0 to 10, where 0 is totally uncomfortable, and 10 is completely, totally comfortable.

Now, completely withdraw your attention from your friend. Listen with your ears, but with your body ignore them. Physically turn your body so it faces away from them. Turn your head away from them. Look at your watch. Most importantly, think about other things: what you have to do tomorrow, what you are going to do on the weekend. A warning – this may feel quite uncomfortable, but it is important that you completely withdraw your attention. Now ask your friend how good they felt about the conversation on a scale of 0 to 10.

Now, pay complete attention to your friend. Turn your body to face them. Hang on to their every word as if this was the most important and interesting conversation that you have ever experienced. Shut out the rest of the world. Pretend there is a huge spotlight on your friend, making them your complete focus. Now ask how good they felt about the conversation on a scale of 0 to 10. Write this down.

Compare the scores. You will be amazed at the differences. Ask your friend and see how they were feeling when you were listening. Compare this to when you withdrew your attention.

Step 2

This is the most important part of the exercise. This time you are going to be talking and experiencing the power of listening.

Your friend has to completely withdraw their attention from you. Just as you did, they need to turn away. They need to look at their watch. They need to think about other things. They need to pretend that this is the most boring conversation that they have ever heard. They need to look around the room – everywhere except at you. Talk for a while. How does this look and feel? How enjoyable is the conversation on a scale of 0 to 10? Write this down.

Now your friend must pay complete attention to you. They must turn their body to completely face you. They need to treat this conversation as if it was the most interesting topic in the world. They need to pretend that there is a huge spotlight above your head making you their complete and total focus. Talk for a while – how does this look, sound and feel? Rate how enjoyable the conversation is on a scale of 0 to 10. Write this down.

Compare your scores. You will see the amazing difference that listening makes.

In summary:

- People who flirt are more successful – their key skill is listening to the people with whom they are flirting.
- Listening is the most powerful tool in your flirting arsenal.
- People love to be listened to – it makes them feel important.
- If you listen to someone, they will be more focused and they will think of you in a positive light.
- If you don't listen, people will feel infuriated, worthless, angry and think of you very negatively.
- Listen to a person and you will boost their positive impression of you.

Making people feel important

The crucial fact about listening is that when you are paying attention to someone, you are making them feel important.

One of my listening skills workshops takes place in a doctor's surgery where they are busy, constantly pushed for time, with too many patients and not enough staff. One of the biggest problems that they faced was that staff were just not listening to each other.

With this group, as with many others, it is interesting to note that most people think that they are really good listeners. The first step in the exercise I did with this group was that people had to completely focus on the other person – treat the conversation as if it was the most important conversation in the world. Immediately once they started talking, there was a real buzz in the room. Conversation was loud, people were laughing – when the exercise was brought to a halt, people were really genuinely reluctant to stop.

The people who were being listened to found the conversation really, really easy. Most of their scores were high with 9s and 10s. Then came the more compelling part of the exercise: asking these people how they felt during the conversation: valued, important, listened to.

One person said 'I didn't want to stop,' 'as a district nurse, usually I do all the listening, it was wonderful to be listened to!'

Listening made these people feel important. By focusing your complete attention on someone, by listening to what they are saying, you are essentially making them feel important. And there is almost nothing else in the world that people like more than to feel important.

It was also very interesting during the second part of the exercise where people completely removed their attention from the person they were speaking to. They turned their chairs away, turned their bodies away, and were instructed to pretend they were paying attention, but they were really doing other things, like looking at their mobile phones or thinking about the weekend.

The effect was dramatic. The sound and tone of the conversation in the room dropped dramatically. The volume was much lower and the sound less rambunctious. The exercise had to be halted early because many people had stopped speaking to each other.

Again, people were asked how easy the conversation was when the other person had withdrawn their attention. The results were startling with low scores of 0 or 1. When people were asked how they felt when the other person wasn't listening, they answered: 'Angry', 'Upset', 'I wanted to stop', 'I wasn't interested in talking to them', 'Unimportant', 'Undervalued', 'Dismissed'. The overwhelming finding was that when someone else didn't listen to them, it made them feel unimportant – it took away their importance and made them feel small.

Though this is not a scientific sample, almost all of the group felt that it was ten times easier to talk to someone when they were listening intently! These same people, who all knew each other and who had been having the same conversation, went from feeling important, happy and valued to the complete polar opposite, simply because the person they talked to had stopped listening and had withdrawn their attention.

There is a crucial lesson here for your flirting skills. You must listen because listening makes people feel important.

Exercise

During the next conversation you have, pretend that this person is the most important person in the world. Imagine that there is a huge spotlight on them. Imagine a huge sign above their heads in flashing lights saying 'Make me feel important'. Completely focus all of your attention on them and on what they are saying.

Then take notice of what happened. How did the conversation feel? What did it sound like? Did you get a feel for how differently the person reacted to you?

The essence of flirting every day is to make every single person that you meet feel important. It is about giving them your complete attention and listening to them. What you will find is that there will be a dramatic difference in how people react to you. Just the simple act of paying complete attention and making someone feel important will hugely magnify how positively people react to you.

In summary:

- Most people think they are good listeners – most people aren't.
- By focusing your complete attention on a person, you are making them feel important – this is crucial in flirting.
- Withdraw your attention and you will have the opposite effect – people will feel unimportant, undervalued, dismissed and angry.
- Focusing your complete attention on people will make it much easier for people to talk to you.

People in relationships flirt too

One perception that I would heartily like to dismiss is that flirting is something that is solely used for finding a partner. It is annoying that flirting often has negative connotations, something that people do to manipulate others. This is untrue – everyday flirting is essentially about being interested in other people and making them feel important.

The key issue is that there is a division between flirting with intent and just flirting for fun. To put it bluntly, if you are flirting with someone and you would like the relationship to become sexual, then you are flirting with intent. If you are simply enjoying an interaction with someone, paying complete attention to them and making them feel good, then you are enjoying simple everyday flirting. The danger here is that some people may interpret being friendly and interested to mean that you are sexually interested in them.

The skills that I talked of earlier are about flirting for fun. This is the type of flirting that people who have a spouse or partner do. Just by listening to someone, you are flirting; the key is to realize the difference between sexual flirting signals and social flirting signals. One of the easiest ways to draw this distinction early on is by making it clear that you are taken. If someone's flirting has gone from social flirting to sexual flirting, draw a clear line. You can learn to do this quite easily. It is very, very simple. As soon as you see, hear or feel that the person you are flirting with has stepped into sexual flirting, mention a girlfriend or boyfriend. Usually it is pretty easy to slip it into the conversation somewhere.

If you think back on it, I am sure you will have noticed when a person drew this sort of flirting line with you. Or perhaps there has been a time when you have had to draw this sort of flirting line with another person. Women are particularly good at drawing the flirting line, usually because they have to practise it as men tend to be a little slow on the uptake, thinking that friendly flirting is sexual flirting.

If you think that a person is starting sexual flirting with you and you have a partner, then you must draw the line. You must make it clear that you are unavailable.

In Chapter 7, you will learn about flirting body language in order to know whether a person fancies you or not. Also, pay attention to your own body language – it is important to be able to withdraw your flirting signals if someone is pushing over the line.

The great thing is that once you have made it clear that you are unavailable, you can go back to flirting with the person. You can listen to them, have fun and be a bit cheeky. There is a reason why women have so much fun with gay men – there has been a clear line drawn in the sand. They both know that nothing is going to happen between them, so they can flirt and have all the fun they want. Actually, you may have noticed that when you see women with gay men they often seem quite flirtatious – well they are! When you draw the line clearly with someone, often it lets you have a little more fun with flirting. They know that you are unavailable, so you can both relax.

The crucial thing to remember is that people who are in a relationship can flirt too. In fact, they often seem to flirt more than people who are single! When you are in a relationship, draw a clear line in the sand; make it clear that you are not available for sexual flirting, then sit back and have some fun!

In summary:

- Flirting is about having fun and making other people feel important.
- People in relationships flirt too.
- There is a difference between social flirting and sexual flirting.
- Make sure you draw a line in the sand – tell the other person that you are already taken.

04 major flirting illnesses

In this chapter you will learn:
- if you are suffering from any of the most common 'flirting illnesses'
- what you can do about 'flirting illnesses'
- what impact 'flirting illnesses' have on your flirting.

Most people are actually single for a reason. Often they have a small piece of the dating and flirting jigsaw missing. When you find out what that piece of the jigsaw is and then you put the piece in place, your flirting will finally also click into place.

Case study

Lucy and Sarah were both friendly and open and found it quite easy to meet people. Yet for some reason they never really managed to find the types of men they wanted. So where were they going wrong? They were a classic case of having a piece of the flirting jigsaw missing. They were both excellent at giving off friendly flirting signals, that is opening conversations, taking an interest in someone, making them feel important and listening. What they lacked was the sexy side of flirting. They simply never escalated their flirting signals beyond 'friendship'.

We worked together, and they learned sexy flirting signals, which you will learn later, in chapter 6. The results were brilliant. One of them, who had not been on a date for years, promptly had several dates lined up. The other got together with an old flame. It was simply that they both had a piece of the flirting jigsaw missing and needed it put in place.

Case study

Jenny had pretty much everything in place, but she was suffering from bastarditis – being attracted to the wrong sort of man over and over again. We worked together to change the types of men she was attracted to. Once the new piece of the jigsaw was in place, everything came together. She has now found a new man, who is definitely not a bastard, and they recently got married.

The next section is about seeing whether you have one of the pieces of the flirting puzzle missing. I call these pieces 'flirting illnesses', since it is an easy way to classify what are often quite common problems.

Many people don't know where they are going wrong. Flirting seems too hard because they feel that they are fumbling around in the dark. Once they actually know what is wrong, for instance, they have 'frienditis' or perhaps 'signal failure', it is as if they have turned the light on. If you know what is ailing you, you can treat it, and that allows you to move forward.

In summary:

- People are usually single for a reason – they have a piece of the flirting puzzle missing.
- If someone is giving off the wrong signals, they won't get anywhere.
- A few tweaks can make a big difference – put the piece back in the flirting puzzle and suddenly you get the full picture.

Flirting and dating illnesses

For each of the 'flirting and dating illnesses' you will find below a description of the ailment and some guidelines on possible cures. For the most common illnesses, you will be able to use the mind programming CD that is included with this book. For most people, it is all very well to read something, but what is really needed is action and to change your behaviour.

Time after time I notice that I can talk to my clients, but they don't actually change what they do. How many friends do you have like this? You've already given them advice on the mistakes they make over and over again in their relationships. They listen to you sincerely, they agree, and then they do exactly the same thing again.

We are creatures of habit. We have a particular way of doing things, and often with good reason. For instance, the women in the first case study opposite were not giving off sexy flirting signals for a reason – the signals meant risking hurt and rejection. However, this meant that they threw out the baby with the bathwater!

This is where the mind programming CD comes in – it includes techniques that will quickly help to reprogramme your brain and your behaviour. Though people are creatures of habit, the amazing thing is that, given the right set of circumstances, they will change their behaviour rapidly. It only takes one set of the right circumstances, and their behaviour will change forever.

To give an interesting example, Jim was bitten quite badly by a dog as a child. Instantly, from that moment on, he was afraid of dogs. It was a pattern that continued throughout his life. Using the same patterns that his brain used in the first place, it was possible to quickly and easily change his feelings about dogs. In fact, later he walked by a big bull terrier and just smiled at it! He didn't even think about it, the dog looked so friendly. Before he would have been terrified.

The results of the mind programming techniques are not always this instant but by using them you will start to change your behaviour, and most importantly how you feel, see and talk about a particular situation or issue.

I often use these mind programming techniques with my clients. In fact, every time a person comes to see me face to face, they take home a CD with some of these techniques to use for their homework. It is like having a little date doctor that they can access at any time. I have found that some of the most dramatic and best changes have come from people using these CDs, which is why I have included one with this book.

In summary:

• Dating illnesses have symptoms and there is action that you can take.
• The mind programming CD will help you to change your behaviour and the way you think.
• We are largely creatures of habit, we often read, but don't take action.
• Given the right set of circumstances, your brain will change the way you act quickly and easily.
• I frequently use the mind programming techniques with clients.

Signal failure

One of the most common flirting ailments is signal failure. What is interesting about signal failure is that different cultures seem to have different versions of the ailment. For instance, the British seem to find it particularly difficult to show interest in someone that they fancy. The Americans, on the other hand, seem to show interest in everyone. Australians come across as just being friendly.

So what is all this signal stuff? The easiest way to understand it is that we are all walking around with a big traffic light over our head. For each person we see, the traffic light either shows:

• red – not interested
• orange – maybe, get ready for action
• green – I fancy you, come over and have a chat.

The signals given through our body language or, more specifically, through eye contact – is a subject that is mentioned by many flirt experts, but curiously something that is mentioned only in passing. The experts mention that if someone is interested, they will give you three seconds' eye contact. Then they will look back a second time. From my practical experience down in the trenches of the flirting war zone, eye contact is one of the biggest minefields. The amount of eye contact that people give varies enormously, based on the city in which you live, the country from where you come and, of course, your personality. This then gives rise to an enormous amount of confusion. Women may think they are giving a green light, and men won't be sure.

This whole issue hit home when I was running workshops in London on giving eye contact. I realized that although the material on eye contact said that three seconds of eye contact was a green light, in London this was enormously difficult.

At a singles night, I gathered together 20 men and women. They were placed on either side of the room, and each person was allocated a person to give their green light to. Just telling people how long to hold their stare is not enough – when I told the women three seconds, it looked to the men like it was three microseconds. Amazingly, to the women it felt like it was ten minutes.

The comments from the women went like this: 'Oh my god that felt weird', 'I must look like a crazy person', 'Now he knows I'm begging for it', 'That felt like ages and ages'. To this, the men responded: 'That was really quick', 'I missed that', 'Was that a green light?'

It is crucial to get the timing exactly right. We changed tack, and I asked the women in the group to look across at the men and say in their head 'You … are really fit'. This is a particularly British saying. For Australians, to be fit just means you jog a lot and go to the gym. In Britain it means attractive, gorgeous, hot, etc. My first attempts at 'You are really hot' failed miserably as the women descended into fits of giggles.

Once the women started doing this so that it felt like they were talking slowly in their heads – looking at the guy they fancied, catching his eye directly, saying (inside their head), 'You are really gorgeous', then looking away – suddenly everything changed.

'That is definitely a green light!', 'Oh yeah', etc came from the men. Timing is crucial. Eye contact can't be too short, because men won't realize that women are giving them a green light. However, it can't be too long. Historically, eye contact is an extremely powerful body language signal. Researchers have found that people who are in love spend more than 70 per cent of the time staring into each other's eyes, making direct eye contact. Conversely, between men, extended eye contact is a signal of aggression. Monkeys are the same – prolonged eye contact between males either leads to one male looking away and submitting or it leads to combat.

Women often feel uncomfortable giving prolonged eye contact. However, what feels to them like a really long time, actually looks on the outside like a short time. In workshops, when women practise on each other rather than on men, the same pattern emerges. The woman giving the eye contact says 'Oh that was ages' and the woman receiving the eye contact says 'That was really quick!'

After much trying and testing, having women looking at men and saying to themselves 'You are really gorgeous' has proved to be the perfect balance between long enough – so the men see the green signal – and short enough so the women don't look like desperate money grabbers.

In summary:

- One of the most common flirting ailments is signal failure.
- We send flirting signals through our body language.
- The amount of eye contact that women give varies enormously.
- To give a green signal to a man, a woman should hold eye contact and say 'You are really gorgeous!' in their head, and then repeat. Eye contact shouldn't be any longer than this or it could be perceived as intimidating.

Signal failure in women

So, now you know that you have to give eye contact to show interest, let's talk about signal failure in women. One of the most common issues for women is that they give a red light to men they fancy.

I can't show him I'm interested

Women see a man that they fancy and immediately they look away. Often they actually physically turn their backs away. This is some of the most extreme body language that you can give someone to show that you are not interested. Essentially, not only are they showing a red light, they are putting up a big 'go away' sign.

Why does this happen? Well, there are two reasons. The first is that women don't want the man to know that they are interested. This is, of course, crazy! You like him, so show interest! However, many women are scared of rejection.

This is closely connected to the second reason – women may feel that it is the man's job to approach them. They may want the man to make the first move. This leads me to one of the biggest myths that surrounds flirting – that it is the men who do all the hunting.

Women are the choosers

One of the great myths of flirting is that men are the hunters. In fact if you look at the research, it is women who are the hunters – about 70 per cent of the time it is the women who do the *selecting*. It is crucial that you understand this – it is the women who select the men they want, and then the men who take action. Essentially a woman's job is to give a green light and a man's job is to do something about it.

For some women this is uncomfortable because they want the men to select them. Well, just think of it this way, if you went to a shop, would you prefer some random stranger to choose your clothes? Or would you prefer to select your clothes yourself?

Some women say they are scared of giving green lights and that they are scared of the possible rejection. Yet what would she feel like if she had to cross the room and start a conversation with every man that she fancied? How much more embarrassing would that be? As a woman, you might be squealing 'I could never do that', but that is exactly what men have to do almost every single time. Think of how much easier it is to catch someone's eye than it is to have to walk all the way across a room and start a conversation. Really, women have it easy. Women get to select their partners. For the men, it is about spotting the women who have selected them, and then taking the long walk across the room or the bar.

For men, it is crucial that they understand this point – women do the selecting. Otherwise, you are driving in the dark. Once you realize that 70 per cent of the time it is the women who do the selecting, it will make your flirting so much easier. You need to learn to spot the green lights from them, and you will get a friendly reception most of the time, unless there is something wrong with the woman's signals.

Generally, women who have signal failure fall into one of three categories. They have either green light failure, signal reversal or red light jam.

Green light failure

This is when women feel uncomfortable showing that they are interested in a person. Usually, when they fancy someone, they immediately turn away, blush, or feel that there is no way that they want to show the person that they are interested. Somehow, miraculously, they expect the men they fancy to read their minds in spite of the negative body language they are showing. How can you tell if you have green light failure? Normally, you will notice one or more of the following:

- Men who you fancy don't come and talk to you.
- You feel shy and turn away from men that you fancy.
- You feel uncomfortable with the idea of showing a man that you are interested in him.

Signal reversal

This is another interesting variation on signal failure. Essentially, these women give green lights to everyone who they don't fancy, but give red lights to the men that they do like. How can you tell if you have signal reversal? One or more of the following factors will apply to you:

- You are a people-watcher.
- People who you don't want to talk to often come up and start a conversation with you, particularly bums, drunks and strangers.
- You feel uncomfortable showing interest in someone you fancy.
- It feels as if you have a big sign around your neck saying 'come and chat with me' (which you do by the way).

For you, the section on people-watching without getting caught (page 36) is crucial.

Red light jam

The women that have a red light jam have their lights permanently on red. They generally don't get approached by anyone, particularly not the men that they fancy. How can you tell if you have red light jam? You will notice one or more of the following:

- People describe you as cold and unapproachable, even though you don't necessarily feel this way.

- Very few or no people approach you.
- They only way you tend to meet people is through introductions from friends or work colleagues.
- Even when you do fancy someone, they never seem to notice.
- The only people who approach you are married or are womanizers.

So what can I do?

Before you start reading this section, make sure you are somewhere quiet and that you have a CD player or MP3 player with all the material from the CD with you and a pen.

Do you recognize any of the symptoms mentioned above? Do you fit into one particular category? Generally, there is a simple cure. You need to become comfortable with giving eye contact to someone that you fancy. This is an easy thing to say, but in reality some women often find this quite a challenge. There are many good reasons why some women are shy about not giving eye contact to someone they fancy. They may believe that it is the man's job to do the hunting. They may live in a big city where, culturally, eye contact is strongly discouraged. They may be scared of rejection. In all of these cases, essentially you have a document stored in your brain that says: *Eye contact with someone I fancy* – Bad; to be avoided.

What we are going to do is rewrite this document so that every time your brain accesses it, it will say: *Eye contact with someone I fancy* – Good; feels, looks and sounds comfortable.

This is where the mind programming CD that comes with the book comes into play. We are going to take your current document about eye contact, and cut and paste positive feelings, images and sounds from another document into it. To do this, we need to search through the other documents in your brain and get them ready for use!

Making eye contact comfortable – Exercise

Right now, think of something that makes you feel fantastic. For some people, it may be dancing, for some of my clients it is eating chocolate, for others it is bungee jumping or walking in the mountains. Now I want you to think of something that made you feel the most fantastic you can remember. On a scale of 0 to 10, where 0 is nothing and 10 is the most amazing you can ever remember feeling, this must be as close to 10 as possible. Sometimes, people can only think of a 5 or an 8. That's okay too, but it must be the best memory that you can remember right now.

Right now, write down the thing that makes you feel really, really fantastic.

....

....

Right now, write down the specific time when you were doing this thing that made you feel really, really fantastic.

....

....

Right now, remember the specific time that made you feel really, really fantastic and write down what you saw, through your own eyes.

....

....

Right now, remember the specific time that made you feel really, really fantastic and write down what you heard, through your ears.

....

....

Right now, remember the specific time that made you feel really, really fantastic and write down how you felt, the sensations you had inside your body.

....

....

Right now, think about giving someone you fancy eye contact. Think about how it looks, sounds and feels. Circle how comfortable you are with giving eye contact on a scale of 0 to

10 where 0 is totally uncomfortable and 10 is totally comfortable. Remember this score.

0   1   2   3   4   5   6   7   8   9   10

Right now, write down how you feel about yourself and talk to yourself when giving someone you fancy eye contact.

....

....

Right now, play the CD and listen to track 1 – making eye contact comfortable.

When you have finished listening to the CD, think about giving someone you fancy eye contact. Think about how it looks, sounds and feels. Circle how comfortable you are with giving eye contact on a scale of 0 to 10 where 0 is totally uncomfortable and 10 is totally comfortable.

0   1   2   3   4   5   6   7   8   9   10

Right now, put the CD on once more, and listen to track 1 again. Now you have finished listening to the CD again, think about giving someone you fancy eye contact. Think about how it looks, sounds and feels. Circle how comfortable you are with giving eye contact on a scale of 0 to 10 where 0 is totally uncomfortable and 10 is totally comfortable.

0   1   2   3   4   5   6   7   8   9   10

Right now, put the CD on yet again, and listen to track 1. Now you have finished listening to the CD once more, think about giving someone you fancy eye contact. Think about how it looks, sounds and feels. Circle how comfortable you are with giving eye contacton a scale of 0 to 10 where 0 is totally uncomfortable and 10 is totally comfortable.

0   1   2   3   4   5   6   7   8   9   10

Right now, put the CD on again, and listen to track 1 one more time. Now you have finished listening to the CD, think about giving someone you fancy eye contact. Think about how it looks, sounds and feels. Circle how comfortable are you with giving eye contact on a scale of 0 to 10 where 0 is totally uncomfortable and 10 is totally comfortable. Compare this to your first score.

0   1   2   3   4   5   6   7   8   9   10

Right now, write down how you look at, feel about and talk to yourself when giving someone you fancy eye contact. Compare these thoughts with your old thoughts on the previous page.

....

....

Congratulations! You have now started to re-programme your mind to be more comfortable with eye contact. You might need to repeat listening to the CD a couple of times. Keep repeating the exercise until you feel you are comfortable enough to make eye contact.

People-watching without getting caught

Being able to check out a guy without getting caught is a crucial skill for all women to master. You have to make sure you fancy him before you can decide if you are going to give him a green light or not! Here is a very simple and very effective technique for checking out guys without getting caught. Some of you may already be using this technique, and if so congratulations! You are already ahead of the game.

The key is to use your peripheral vision. Most women are really quite good at using their peripheral vision – certainly better then men, who generally tend to use the 'stare and gawp' technique. For the men reading this, it should be very instructive for you. Despite appearances to the contrary, women are actually checking out men all the time – the key is that they are not getting caught.

In summary:

- Checking out men without being noticed is a crucial skill for women.
- Women actually check out men all the time.
- The trick is to use your peripheral vision so you don't get caught!

Peripheral vision exercise – using your hand

Using peripheral vision means you can see what people are doing without looking directly at them or, more specifically, without making eye contact with them. You can discreetly check out someone without them ever seeing a green light or without them even knowing you have been doing it.

Right now, hold up your left hand in front of you at head level. Move it to the left of your centre of vision. Have your palm facing towards you. Now look straight ahead.

What you are looking at should look like this:

Focus here

Figure 1

Look where the cross is and notice what you can see about your hand with your peripheral vision. You will actually see quite a lot. You can tell that it is a hand; you can tell that you have five fingers; you can tell the size of the hand; and, very importantly, you can tell that your palm is facing towards you.

Now, while you are still looking to the centre of your field of vision, turn your hand sideways. Watch the movement with your peripheral vision.

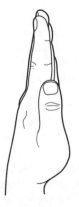

Focus here

Figure 2

What can you see about your hand with your peripheral vision now? Again you can't see the clear specific details, like your fingernails, or the details of the creases in your hand, but you can see that your hand is turned to the side, and other important details like how far it has turned.

Now, looking at the centre, turn your hand so that your palm faces you, and then back again, keep doing this. With your peripheral vision, you can easily notice the movement, and easily see if your palm is facing towards you, or whether your palm is facing to the side.

So, what has all this got to do with flirting? Well, you can do exactly the same with the men or women that you are checking out. You can use your peripheral vision to check out exactly in which direction they are looking. Then, when they are looking away, you can check them out in detail. As soon as you see them turning towards you, you can turn your eyes away and avoid eye contact.

In summary:

- Peripheral vision allows you to check someone out without making eye contact.
- Practise looking at your hand using peripheral vision.
- You can use your peripheral vision to check out exactly where a person is looking.
- When a person looks away, you can check them out without giving a green light.

Peripheral vision exercise in the field

Now that you have practised the peripheral vision exercise at home, it is time to get out in the field and try it. When you go out today, try the peripheral vision exercise on people. Start on members of the same sex to begin with – there is less chance that they will think you are trying to pick them up. Choose a person. Look at them using your peripheral vision. See how much you can notice about them. Notice if they are turning their head towards you, or away from you. Once they turn their heads away, check them out directly. If they start to turn towards you, flick your eyes away and keep looking at them with your peripheral vision.

This is a crucial skill for women to master in order to check out which men they should give green lights to, without everyone they are looking at coming over and chatting them up. It is really easy once you get the hang of it. Generally, it only takes about five minutes of practice for women to really get the whole concept of peripheral vision.

For people-watching women, who give green lights to everyone, this really is a bonus, and a bit of a revelation! They get to people-watch without the bums, losers and drunks coming and chatting them up. All the benefits without any of the problems. They need to experience using their peripheral vision and, once they have, there is no turning back.

You will also find that, with a little practice, using your peripheral vision becomes second nature. At first you will need to think about it but, like with everything else, the more you use it, the quicker it will become automatic. I have noticed that women seem to be particularly good at using their peripheral vision. For men, it seems to take a little more practice. Most men are so used to just staring that it takes a little extra work, but it is well worth it. If you stare, women tend to think you are either creepy or weird!

A final warning for men – don't practice this exercise on tough looking male characters. As I mentioned before, staring and eye contact are signs of aggression. If a man catches you looking, he could take it badly. Be selective about the people you choose to practise on. Better still, just practise on women; they are used to men staring at them!

In summary:

- Try the peripheral vision exercise out on people.
- Start the exercise with a member of the same sex.
- Practise spotting if people are looking away from you or at you.
- Peripheral vision is particularly useful if you are a people-watcher.
- With a little practice, using peripheral vision will become second nature.
- Be selective about who you practise on!

Signal failure in men

Signal failure in men tends to come in two forms:

1 Men just don't see the signals.
2 Men give contradictory signals to women.

Signal blindness

Signal blindness is one of the most common ailments among men. One of the early questions men should ask themselves is whether they can tell if a woman would like them to go and talk to her.

If you are a man, ask yourself this question – when you walk into a bar, party or pub, can you tell which women are interested in you? Can you see the ones who would like to talk with you? How do you know they are interested? The signals that women give off are amazingly simple. The way that a woman gives a green signal is through eye contact. She will look, catch your eye (orange light), then usually look again within about a minute and catch your eye again (green light).

It seems terribly obvious, but the first thing you have to do is look for these signals. In some ways, not surprisingly, most men don't even see these signals because they are not looking at the eyes. Let's focus, for example, on the issue of green lights and looking for eye contact. The first thing that a woman does if she is interested is make eye contact, and that eye contact is usually relatively quick.

Walk through any bar and note the women that are making eye contact with you. You'll be amazed that so many are making eye contact. If you've never noticed this before, perhaps you've been too busy looking elsewhere.

This may seem a little crude, but women tend to check out men from the top down. That is, they look at their face and eyes and then check out the rest of a man's assets. A man does exactly the opposite. He starts from the bottom, looks up, and then moves on to the woman's face.

Imagine a race with both sexes starting at the same time. When the woman is giving her green signal and looking for eye contact, most men are looking completely in the wrong direction. It takes a little retraining, but men must look around the room and check out women's faces first. The women will be doing the same, so this is your best chance to catch them giving you a green light. You can leave the rest to later.

So, men actually don't bother to look for the signals at the right time. This is like driving in rush hour traffic and looking at the road all the time without bothering to look up at the traffic lights. Crazy. You are going to miss all the crucial signals. In flirting, this is like driving blind.

In summary:

- Signal blindness is one of the most common flirting ailments in men.
- Can you tell which women are interested in you? If not, you suffer from signal blindness.
- You have to be looking for the signals to see them!
- Men get distracted by looking at women's bodies rather than at their faces and eyes.
- Men tend to look at women from the bottom up.
- As a man, you need to retrain yourself to look at a woman's face first – that way you are more likely to spot a green signal!

Does she really want me to come and talk to her?

Often, men spot the signals women send out, but are not really sure of what they mean. Single men may struggle to believe that getting a green light from a woman is as simple as getting double eye contact. Really, it is just as simple as a green light when you are driving, and means exactly the same thing. Go, get moving!

'What if she just made eye contact by mistake?', 'I'm not sure if it was long enough' etc. These are often what the men say who are not sure about the signals.

You can be totally sure that there is no way that a woman will make eye contact with you once (orange signal), and then make eye contact with you a second time (green signal) by mistake. Men, if a woman catches your eye twice, she is sending you a very simple signal – 'You look interesting, come and talk to me'. Get moving and go and talk to her.

Red lights from men

In the same way that women sometimes give red lights to the men they fancy when they are having signalling problems, men can do the same thing. Since a green signal is made up of two glances, you have to be looking for the second glance from the woman. Many men actually look away and don't look back if they get a first glance from a woman. That way, they do not see the crucial second glance and their green signal!

In many ways, it is just like the female version of signal failure. Most commonly, men say to me that they don't want to feel like they are staring at the woman. They don't want to appear like a sleaze or a stalker. If you stare for hours continuously and drool, then you are a stalker! Men need some techniques to make them feel comfortable with keeping an eye on a woman while looking for the green light second glance.

There are reasons to feel uncomfortable if you keep staring at a woman when she has first made eye contact. Eye contact can be perceived as highly aggressive, but it is also a sign of interest – you are literally showing a woman that you fancy her.

So, guys, you need to learn how to use your peripheral vision. Peripheral vision is vastly underused by men. Men are rather direct creatures. In the same way that most men think that they are being subtle when they are checking out a woman's cleavage, but women pick it up a mile away, men often have not been trained in the art of using peripheral vision.

For women, I have shown you how to use your peripheral vision to check out men without making eye contact. For men, there is a subtle twist on this. You can keep an eye on a woman you are hoping to get a green signal from, or one who has already caught your eye once, using your peripheral vision. You can keep an eye on her without staring directly.

Case study

Adrian had never had much luck with spotting whether women liked him. He had particularly noticed several women that he fancied on his regular train ride to work. Adrian felt uncomfortable looking directly for eye contact, so I worked with him using his peripheral vision. Much to his surprise he discovered that the woman that he fancied was actually checking him out quite often. Using his peripheral vision, he spotted when she was looking at him and made eye contact, getting a green light. After a couple of green lights, he worked up the courage to get a conversation going. He was delighted and surprised at how friendly she was and they ended up exchanging phone numbers.

The key is to keep an eye on a woman without staring directly. Then, using your peripheral vision, you can see when a woman is looking at you. You can then turn and catch her eye.

Look at the X in Photo 1. Now, look with your peripheral vision while you are staring at the X and see if you can tell that the girl in the photo is looking away – of course you can.

Photo 1

Now focus on the X below, and look at the girl's face in Photo 2 with your peripheral vision. Can you tell that she is looking at you directly? Of course you can! So this is the moment that you turn and catch her green light!

Photo 2

In summary:

- Men can give red lights to women they fancy by not making eye contact; this is a male version of signal failure.
- Long staring is uncomfortable so men need to learn to use their peripheral vision.

- Use your peripheral vision to keep an eye out for a green signal from a woman you fancy.
- You can keep an eye on a woman without staring directly.
- When a woman turns towards you, catch her eye!

Ultra red – not comfortable making eye contact

This type of signal problem is rarer than most, but very important to fix. Some men are not comfortable with holding eye contact with women at all. This is a real problem. It is like driving with a blindfold on. Men who feel uncomfortable aren't going to get started at all. They are refusing to look for even the most basic flirting signal.

There are various reasons for this. Usually, they are uncomfortable showing that they are interested in a woman because they are scared of rejection. Or perhaps they feel that by giving eye contact they are being too aggressive and will put women off. Often they think that by giving eye contact they will look sleazy. All the reasons boil down to the fact that these men can't spot the most basic signals.

With this particular problem, some men actually feel uncomfortable when they receive the first eye contact from a woman – that is, they get the orange light. They then look away from the woman, which means that there is no chance of catching the crucial second glance, which is giving the green light. It is like sitting at the traffic lights and, as soon as you think that the light is going to turn green, you turn away. Or you refuse to look for green lights at all!

From a flirting perspective, this is shooting yourself in the foot! You are suffering from this disorder if:

- You feel uncomfortable making eye contact.
- You are uncomfortable looking for eye contact from women.
- A woman does make eye contact with you and you look away.
- A woman catches your eye once and you look away and don't look back to see if there is a second glance.

Being comfortable with spotting the signals

Recognize any of the symptoms listed above? If so, it is time that you started getting more comfortable with seeing these signals and seeing that a woman is interested in you. There may be a whole raft of complicated reasons why you are this way, but there seems to be a document in your head that says: *Giving eye contact to women* – Bad, look away!

There are always positive reasons why we do these things. Perhaps you don't want to appear to be a sleaze. Perhaps you are scared of rejection. Perhaps in the past you haven't realized that making eye contact is really important to be able to see the crucial green signals from women. By reprogramming your mind document, the aim is to allow you to keep the positive things and have a better way of getting what you wanted in the first place. The human mind is an amazing thing, and I have found over and over again that when my clients are presented with a better way of getting what they want, they will do it.

For instance, if someone offered you a job where you would get paid twice as much to work half the time, you might be thrilled, but also suspicious. This is for a good reason. One of the crucial things about a job is that it gives you security – which is very important. This is where you get the roof over your head, the food that you eat, the clothes that you wear. Consequently, you may be unsure whether you want to go ahead and take the job. Your friends might be pushing you because, on the face if it, it looks like such a great deal. Yet you would have a good reason to have reservations. What if the job only lasts a couple of months? Then your other job might not be available once you finished. The sensible thing is to find out more about the job – find out if it has the same security as your old job, and delivers what you want. That way you can have your cake and eat it too. Now it's time to give you a nibble of the cake.

Exercise

Right now, think of something that makes you feel fantastic. For some people, it may be dancing, for some of my clients it is eating chocolate, for others it is bungee jumping or walking in the mountains. Now I want you to think of something that made you feel the most fantastic you can remember. On a scale of 0 to 10, where 0 is nothing, and 10 is the most amazing you can ever remember feeling, this must be as close to 10 as possible. Sometimes, people can only think of a 5 or an 8. That's okay too, but it must be the best memory that you can remember right now.

Right now, write down the thing that makes you feel really, really great.

....

....

Right now, write down the specific time when you were doing this thing that made you feel really, really great.

....

....

Right now, remember the specific time that made you feel really, really great and write down what you saw, through your own eyes.

....

....

Right now, remember the specific time that made you feel really, really great and write down what you heard, through your own ears.

....

....

Right now, remember the specific time that made you feel really, really great and write down how you felt, the sensations you had inside your body.

....

....

Right now, think about giving someone you fancy eye contact. Think about how it looks, sounds and feels. Circle how comfortable you are with giving eye contact on a scale of 0 to 10 where 0 is totally uncomfortable and 10 is totally comfortable. Remember this score.

0   1   2   3   4   5   6   7   8   9   10

Right now, write down how you feel about yourself and talk to yourself when giving someone you fancy eye contact.

....

....

Right now, play the CD and listen to track 1.

When you have finished listening to the CD, think about giving someone you fancy eye contact. Think about how it looks, sounds and feels. Circle how comfortable you are with giving eye contact on a scale of 0 to 10 where 0 is totally uncomfortable and 10 is totally comfortable.

0   1   2   3   4   5   6   7   8   9   10

Right now, listen to track 1 again.

When you have finished listening to the CD again, think about giving someone you fancy eye contact. Think about how it looks, sounds and feels. Circle how comfortable you are with giving eye contact on a scale of 0 to 10 where 0 is totally uncomfortable and 10 is totally comfortable.

0   1   2   3   4   5   6   7   8   9   10

Right now, listen to track 1 once more. Then think about giving someone you fancy eye contact. Think about how it looks, sounds and feels. Circle how comfortable you are with giving eye contact on a scale of 0 to 10 where 0 is totally uncomfortable and 10 is totally comfortable.

0   1   2   3   4   5   6   7   8   9   10

Right now, listen to track 1 again one more time. When you have finished listening to the CD, think about giving someone you fancy eye contact. Think about how it looks, sounds and feels. Circle how comfortable you are with giving eye contact on a scale of 0 to 10 where 0 is totally uncomfortable and 10 is totally comfortable. Compare this to your first score opposite.

0   1   2   3   4   5   6   7   8   9   10

Right now, write down how you feel about yourself and talk to yourself when giving someone you fancy eye contact. Compare these thoughts with your old thoughts.

....

....

Congratulations! You have now started to re-programme your mind to be more comfortable with eye contact. You might need to repeat listening to the CD a couple of times. Keep repeating the exercise until you feel you are comfortable enough to make eye contact.

Ex-itis

An astonishing number of people start trying to flirt when they are still not ready, perhaps after having broken up from a long-term relationship. You break up, you try and move on, you are brave and get out there and start dating. Then someone comes along who you actually really like. Someone who looks like they could be a future potential partner. This somehow manages to bring back all the pain of the break-up, all the memories of how good your last relationship was. And it brings back into focus the risks you are taking here – suddenly the fun bit is over and things are starting to get serious again. There is another chance of getting hurt. This is where people with ex-itis run for the door.

One question I received on a dating website was: 'Sam, I've broken up, it still hurts, is there anything else but time, the great healer, to help me move on?'

This question brings up two interesting issues. First, you have to realize that it *does* take time to get over an ex. Sometimes a long time. People don't realize just how long. I have heard that it takes between a quarter and a half of the time that you were with someone to get over them. So, if you were with someone for ten years, then it should take between 2¹/₂ and 5 years for you to fully recover from your ex-itis. This is a long time, but it makes sense – breaking up leaves you with emotional wounds, and the frustrating thing about emotional wounds is that you can't see them.

If you break your arm, everyone can see what has happened. They are sympathetic. The cast is an external sign of how well, or how badly, you are healing. Once the cast is gone, the people know that you are back to normal. Even then, you might still have a bit of a limp, which will show people where you are up to in the healing process. There are no such casts for relationship break-ups. It's a shame really as it would make a lot of people's lives much easier if there was some sort of external sign to show that you are still getting over a break-up.

The second interesting issue is that, because there are no external signs, people who have broken up with someone are subject to twin pressures. The first pressure is from themselves. Often they feel that they have to move on, and naturally they want to find another partner as quickly as possible to recapture the wonderful thing they had before. The second pressure is from the people who are around them. There is no real rule of thumb about recovery times, no cast to see, and so people around you start pushing to get you in the dating game again. Don't be pushed – give yourself time after a break up.

However, it is possible to accelerate the process of healing. You can move on more quickly from your past relationships and get over ex-itis. Usually I work on a one-to-one basis with my clients on this – it is a complex area and there are quite a few facets to it, too much to cover simply in this book. After all, we are talking about flirting here rather than about exes. So I would make one recommendation. If you are suffering from ex-itis and you would like to get over it much faster, go out and buy yourself a copy of *How to Mend your Broken Heart* by Hugh Willbourn and Paul McKenna. It is packed with loads of useful techniques and could massively reduce the amount of time you need to get over your ex.

It does take time to get over your ex and, if you haven't cured your ex-itis, it can be a serious brake on your flirting. Every time you start getting those lovely green lights, you might find your ex-itis brakes kicking in.

In summary:

- To flirt well, you really need to be over your past relationships.
- It can take a long time to get over an ex – up to half the time you were together.
- A broken arm can be seen, a broken heart can't.
- People feel pressure to move on quickly; friends often push too.
- It is possible to get over exes quickly.

Shopping problems

Another common problem for both men and women is 'shopping'. If you want to go out and buy something, be it a handbag or a new car, you have to shop in the right places. A good analogy for women is that if they want to buy a Prada handbag, then they should be shopping at an upmarket department store, not your local supermarket.

The same goes for the type of man or woman that you are looking for. People are quite interesting. They hang out in packs, often in specific places. What is fascinating about living in a big city, is that whatever you are looking for, if you look hard enough, you will come across people who are looking for the same. Maybe that is a particular martial art, a painting group or a particular style of dancing. If you look in the right places, you will be able to find similar people who have similar interests. Basically, when you have a lot of people gathered together, it provides you with a lot of interesting opportunities.

The same goes for dating. You have to understand the type of person that you are looking for, and then work out the best place in which to find them. It is really a little like shopping.

Think about when you go shopping. When you leave the house, you usually have a clear idea of what you are after and you go to specific shops to get what you want. You wouldn't go to an electronic shop to buy clothes! Or to a clothes shop to buy your groceries!

This is a very simple idea – to find what you want, you have to know what you are looking for and get out and shop for it. What stuns me is how many people ignore this basic rule when dealing with flirting and dating. Somehow they expect their partner to magically appear in front of them. 'It should just happen', 'I know I'll meet them', 'That's a bit clinical, true love should just happen', etc.

Case study

Brooke hadn't had a date for almost a year. On closer questioning, it turned out that she hadn't actually really been out shopping for men for almost a year. No wonder Brooke hadn't had any dates! Would you expect a handbag to magically appear if you never went out to a shop, or took the time online to make the purchase? No, of course not! Yet Brooke seemed mystified by the fact that she hadn't had any dates. She didn't flirt with men in the street, she didn't go speed-dating, she wasn't looking on the internet, and most of her friends were all coupled off. We got her shopping in the right places, and within a month she had her first date.

If you already know what sort of partner you are looking for, and you are out there shopping in the right places, you can skip this section, or perhaps keep on reading in any case because you might think of some other useful places to look for people to flirt with.

In summary:

- People hang out in packs – you can find 'shops' full of particular types.
- You need to know the type of person you are looking for.
- You need to be persistent and find the right shop.
- It won't just happen; you need to know what you are looking for and get out and shop.
- No dates or flirting? Chances are you haven't been out shopping.

What am I looking for?

The first key question when shopping for a partner to flirt with is: what are you looking for? You don't have to make a huge long list (actually modern expectations in relationships are way too high, but that is another matter), instead identify your top three or four essential characteristics.

For example, Sunita, a London journalist I talked to definitely had shopping problems. She complained that she never met the right sort of men. We talked for a while and worked out that her three key required characteristics for a man were:

- Sporty (e.g. rugby, not cricket or tennis)
- Australian
- Professional.

To her, these seemed like just a few simple and quite reasonable characteristics. Well, it was immediately clear why she was having trouble finding a man in London. Although there are Australians in London, they are clearly in a minority. Moreover, as a generalization, most Australians who come to London are not professionals (although this is starting to change somewhat). They have their two-year working visa, go to London, work in a pub, save up their pounds, and then go and have adventures all around Europe. Immediately Sunita is looking for quite a specialist item, a 'Professional Australian in London'. Now, throw into the mix the third and very important characteristic: that they are sporty in a particular type of sport – Sunita liked what could be called 'blokey' games.

Translation: those sports that require quite large muscles and usually involve serious body contact. This narrowed the field even further. Not only was she looking for a very rare breed, she was looking for a rare breed that plays highly physical sports like rugby.

Can you see why Sunita was not meeting any of the men that she liked? They were about as common as dodos, and she was certainly not shopping in places where she might find a dodo.

The next step was to brainstorm about where these rare creatures might be found. The first conclusion was Australia. Blindingly obvious, but very important. Sporty professional rugby playing types are actually quite common in a place like Sydney. However, Sunita wanted to stay in London for the time being, so the brainstorming continued.

Being a journalist, she had the interesting opportunity of being able to cover sporting events. This was more promising. I discovered that, if she asked, she could certainly go along to all the matches where the Australian rugby teams were playing in the UK. Suddenly, she had the ideal gathering places for her ideal man in the UK. Rugby lovers are going to go to rugby games, and Australians are going to go to Australian rugby games. And more likely than not, at those games, you are going to be able to spot the professionals by the types of clothes they are wearing.

'But how do I get to speak to them?' she quite reasonably asked. We used a twist on a technique that is described later in the book – asking for information. She would be working as a journalist at these games, so she could quite reasonably go up to all the men that she fancied and ask them for an interview. And then a beer afterwards.

From there, it was just a matter of talking to her editor about covering more rugby games. The perfect combination: work and shopping, all in one. Sunita had found her specialist man shop.

So, right now, write down the top three characteristics you are looking for in your partner:

1

2

3

This may involve a little thinking, but try to write down the first things that come to mind. You can mix and match, but it is crucial that you work out the top three most important characteristics.

In summary:

- What are your top three or four characteristics you look for in a partner?
- Does this combination of characteristics narrow down or increase your chances?
- If you are looking for a rare species, you need to realize this and do some specialist shopping.
- Work out the places where you might find your ideal man or woman.

Actually shopping

It is crucial that once you know what you are looking for, you actually *look*. Ask yourself this question: when I'm out with friends, shopping, on public transport do I take the time to check out who I find attractive? Many people answer no to this question. They are so busy that they don't actually bother to shop. There are opportunities all around you – you need to open your eyes to them. It would be like going shopping for a handbag and walking straight through the store without actually bothering to look at any of the handbags. Ridiculous! Wherever you are, make sure that you shop – get into the habit of noticing the most attractive people around you. If you don't look, you won't find what you want!

Where to shop

Now you have your top three characteristics, you have to work out where to shop. This can take a little time and effort, but it is well worth it. Be creative about the places that you look.

Lucy, one of my clients, was suffering bastarditis – she was attracted to men who were essentially unavailable, particularly because of their professions. They tended to be the types who were always busy. She was a brilliant client and tried shopping just about everywhere. What was interesting is the lateral place that she found the man that she later married – toy boy speed-dating. If you think about this, it actually makes a lot of sense. Younger men are earlier on in their careers, and so tend to have more time on their hands, especially if they are students or if they have just graduated. If you want to find a man who has some time on his hands, it makes complete sense to look for a younger man.

There are some important things to remember about shopping. Just like the shops, which provide particular types of items and particular levels of quality, there are places that do just the same. The point is that you might not get quantity, but you will get quality. So where are some places to shop?

Case study

Liz was really into sailing. This was something that she really enjoyed and also it tended to fit the type of man that she was looking for – the outdoors type, professional and well advanced in their career. So she joined a bunch of sailing clubs. Though she didn't get the quantity – many of the men were already spoken for – she got the quality. Liz met more eligible men that fitted her criteria than she had in several years.

The internet

The internet is an amazing place – particularly because of the shopping. You can find just about anything that you want, and quickly and easily order it online. But there is also plenty of rubbish on the internet, so you have to be selective.

Internet dating is similar. It is like sticking your hand in a rose bush – you are probably going to get a lot of thorns before you find a rose, unless you are selective with the websites that you use.

Most internet dating websites are really like visiting the supermarket. They have a bit of everything, but not necessarily of the quality you want. There are also now more and more niche dating websites where you can shop for the types of people you want. Into pets? There is a dating website for pet lovers. Rich? There are specific sites for millionaires. Whatever you want, there is probably a website for you.

There are some specific websites that are worth mentioning – they are a breed of website that is more for specialist shopping, rather than nipping down to the supermarket.

www.parship.com

This website is particularly interesting because it uses

psychometric testing to match people. Essentially, this is what your brain is doing anyway when you walk into a party and see someone that you fancy. Your unconscious mind is matching them, their body language, facial features and gestures against all the other people you have met in the past. If they are similar to someone you have fancied in the past, 'bang', you get that feeling of chemistry. This is also tied in with various biological factors, like whether your immune systems are compatible, etc.

After completing a 30-minute questionnaire, you only see people who are similar to you psychologically. The basis of almost all attraction is actually similarity. There is a whole bunch of studies that show that people are attracted to people who are similar to them and tend to have longer, more successful relationships with such people.

This website does the work of sifting through millions of people for you and matching you up with the ones that are most similar to you. Although these people may not quite meet the top three things you are looking for, they will most likely have very similar values and approaches to you. In fact, it is quite likely they will match your criteria because, for instance, you might both be outgoing or sporty.

www.meetup.com

This is a very interesting website because it allows real specialist shopping. Whatever you are into, you will find people on this website who are into something similar. It is not strictly a singles website, but is just for people with similar interests. For example, Jeff was having trouble shopping because he was spending all of his time hanging out with his mates at the local pub. He wasn't meeting any new people, and he wasn't meeting people who had similar interests to him – which included rock music. In fact they played cheesy commercial music in his local pub, which wasn't his cup of tea at all.

A quick search on meetup.com showed that there were 41 rock fans who were also looking to meet up and go to rock gigs. Suddenly from nothing, Jeff had a whole pack of people that shared his interests. And, most importantly, this provided a great hunting ground within the group – he could go with these people to rock gigs, where he was suddenly surrounded by women who shared one of his fundamental interests.

Another client, Claire, somewhat creatively decided that she wanted to shop where there would be very little competition. She thought that there would be a lot of men who were into poker and not many women. She checked out the London Poker Meetup group – 498 members. Man-hunting heaven.

www.mysinglefriend.com

This is one of the first websites that really seems to have cracked the quality issue on the internet. This site is all about quality rather than quanity.

What really makes it unique is that it uses one of the best and oldest ways of finding someone to flirt with – through your friends. The great thing about flirting with a friend of a friend is that they come with a reference. If they know your friend, then you have good reason to believe they are going to be pretty okay. Mysinglefriend.com works on the same basis. The friend of the single person puts them on the website and writes about them. This site taps into the huge pool of people who didn't use internet dating in the past. They are the friend that you can't understand why they are single because they are such a good catch. Often, they are the types who wouldn't normally consider internet dating.

If you are looking for young, successful, good looking and interesting people, this is the website for you.

These websites are all illustrative examples of the sort of online places that you can go to do your specialist shopping. Just about every interest seems to be catered for on the internet, so get googling!

In summary:

- You can buy almost anything on the internet, but you have to be aware there is a lot of rubbish out there.
- Be selective about the internet dating sites you use.
- If you have specific criteria, you can often find a website that will help you to find people who match that group.

Offline

If you are going to shop offline, it is a matter of working out where your preferred type is going to be gathered and then finding a place where they gather. For instance, Jack was looking for an intelligent, artistic type of woman. So I sent him to an art gallery. On his first trip, he got the phone number of a lovely young lady who pretty much fitted his criteria.

I can't tell you all the places to look because there is an infinite combination of criteria and places to look. I can recommend that you treat your searching like a shopping trip at first. Imagine that the partner you want to find is a very specific item.

You need to think about where that item might be available, and particularly where you might find a range of those items so that you have a good choice.

Remember, it might take a while to find the right shop. You are going to have to ask people's advice, and you may have to do some travel. Moreover, there will be many shops on the way that won't quite fit the bill. Be persistent.

Exercise

Right now, write down your top criteria:

1

2

3

Right now, write down a list of people you could ask about places where you might be able to find people with these sorts of criteria:

1

2

3

4

5

Right now, write down places where you might find people who have one or more of these criteria:

1

2

3

4

5

Right now, take one small action towards getting to one of those places. For example, phone one of the people on your list and ask their thoughts. Or hop on the internet and do a google search. Whatever it is, take one small action right now.

Write down, 'The small action I took is …'

It's fine if you haven't filled in all the spaces in the exercise. Your unconscious mind will work on finding places where you can find the type of person you want to flirt with. They will just pop into your mind and you can write them down.

The thing about shopping is that you have to be quite persistent. It is a matter of going to the places you have found and keep working on them. It is also about tailoring your approach to the type of 'shop' you are in.

To illustrate, Pete finds it easier to meet women who are South American and speak Spanish. This is because their cultural signals showing availability tend to be much 'louder' than those of Anglo-Saxons. He is going to try out a Spanish meet-up group. This is quite a large group (there are over 1,500 members), so there should be a good range of people turning up. However, some groups like this tend to be quite stable, in that there is the same core of people who come along again and again. In these cases, it is a matter of going along, checking out the goods available, and if there is no new stock coming in, moving on to some other sort of shop. Just like shopping, you don't go back and keep looking at the same stock, you need to move on to somewhere else.

Other types of shops have an almost continuous turnover. For instance, Jack, the man interested in intelligent artistic types, knows that every single time that he goes to an art gallery, there are going to be new people to meet. Obvious, but again worth pointing out. Sometimes, people are tempted to keep going to the same shop over and over again, despite the lack of stock turnover.

In summary:

• Treat looking for someone to flirt with a little like a shopping trip.
• There are lots of options when shopping.
• Ask people's advice when shopping.
• You will need to be persistent.
• Make sure that your shop has a good stock turnover or find somewhere new!

Rejectaphobia

Rejectaphobia is another common flirting illness that affects both men and women. Simply put, this is when the fear of rejection holds people back in their flirting.

Rejectaphobia in women is most commonly tied to signal failure – a woman is scared of giving off a signal that she is interested in a man because she is scared of rejection. A frequent response to the possibility of giving signals is 'Well, I don't want him to know that I like him' or 'I don't feel comfortable with making it obvious I'm interested' or, sometimes, 'I just get shy around anyone I fancy'.

Case study

Rejectaphobia is as common in shy people as it is in confident people. Let's take Erin, on the outside very confident and extrovert. She is attractive and very successful in her job. Actually, her job requires her to meet and deal with new people: she works in sales. In a professional environment she feels totally comfortable talking to anyone. Yet as soon as she is in a private non-business environment, and it involves someone she fancies, her confidence disappears.

At a dating event she attended, she had managed to talk to almost every single man, except for the two or three that she actually fancied. This was a pattern that repeated itself over and over again – all the events she went to were the same. She had a great night chatting to everyone in the room except for the person she fancied. And why? Because dealing with people at work, she had a kind of business armour on, and when talking to people she didn't fancy, nothing was at stake. Suddenly, if she had to make an approach to someone she really fancied, she were vulnerable – or, more importantly, she was vulnerable to rejection. Despite being a successful, confident, outgoing business woman, she was too scared to give eye contact to someone she really fancied, because if the person didn't reciprocate, then she would feel rejected.

The same problem of rejectaphobia can apply to men, but it is usually easier to spot. Men have to do more of the leg work, so the rejection is much harder. Women can give a signal that they are interested and leave it at that. For a man, he has to make the long walk across the room, and start with an opening line to get the conversation going. Men with rejectaphobia just feel totally uncomfortable about the idea of approaching women or starting a conversation. Often this is with good reason; they have had rejections in the past, and usually the rejections for men are more blatant and painful than not having eye contact returned.

So, girls, please do have some sympathy for men who come and try to flirt with you. It is quite a terrifying experience, so at least be polite and gentle.

In summary:

- Rejectaphobia will hold back your flirting.
- Rejectaphobia is often tied to signal failure.
- Both shy and confident people suffer rejectaphobia.
- Outwardly confident people often don't flirt with the people they really fancy.
- Rejection does hurt, and it is part of the flirting process.
- Ladies, please be polite with men who approach you as it takes a lot of courage.

Taking the pain away

For both men and women, we are essentially dealing with people avoiding the pain of rejection. And with good reason. A tough rejection can really sting you for days afterwards. If it was from someone you fancied, the temptation is to run over it in your head, talking to your self about where it went wrong, and then you are just re-living the pain over and over again.

To be able to deal with rejectaphobia, you need to be able to deal with the pain of rejection. Rejection is going to happen, it is part of the flirting game. Maybe the person you are trying to get eye contact with won't fancy you. Perhaps you will get a green light, start flirting, and then find there is no chemistry. Possibly you only get a few replies from your internet dating. Often you might end up going out on a couple of dates and then things won't go so well. Rejection is there, and if you are going to have any success in flirting, you are going to have to handle some rejection along the way.

What if I told you that I could give you a tablet to take away the rejection pain? Just like when you have a headache, something that is quick to administer and will take the pain away. Let's call this painkiller the 'rejection zapper'. No pharmaceuticals involved though. Only your mind.

When you get rejected, your mind writes a document that says something like: *Chatted to attractive women* – Result, pain of rejection. Or *Gave eye contact to man I fancied* – Result, pain of rejection.

We are going to take a positive memory and use it to zap the rejection memory. The worse the rejection is, the more we will have to zap it.

In summary:

- The key to overcoming rejectaphobia is to be able to get over the pain of rejection quickly and easily.
- Rejection is part of the flirting and dating process: it happens to everyone.
- You can take a painkiller for a headache and it is possible to take away the pain of rejection.
- We are going to take a positive memory and use it to zap the old rejection.

Taking away the pain of rejection

We have pain for a reason – it warns us that we are in some sort of physical danger. For example, if we have cut our finger, we need to get a plaster. Emotional pain often serves a similar purpose. It can warn us that we are doing something emotionally uncomfortable, and try to stop us from repeating the same thing over and over again.

For some things, a certain amount of emotional discomfort is part of the package. To look at it another way, it is something you have to go through to get what you want. A little like physical exercise. When you first go to a gym class it can be really painful – you wheeze during the class and afterwards you ache. Perhaps there are points where you really feel like you want to stop. However, the pain is well worth the reward you get at the end – the buzz from the exercise, the extra energy you will have later in the day, perhaps the weight loss. There is a whole range of benefits that you have to go through some sort of physical discomfort to reach. Eventually, you will reach a point where you realize that this pain is worth the benefits.

It can be the same with flirting and rejection. There may be a little pain to start off with but, in the end, if you get it right, it is worth risking the potential rejection for the great return. After all, you will be meeting an interesting new person, you might even find a long-term partner, or a short-term fling. At least when flirting, you will make the other person and yourself feel good.

It is okay to be worried about the fear of rejection. This exercise will help show you that it is not so bad at all, and can be quickly and easily reduced. So let's start zapping the rejection.

Exercise

Right now, think of a situation that makes you feel really, really great, something that you really enjoy doing. Ideally, this needs to be as near to a 10 as possible on a scale of 0 to 10. For some of my clients, it is the amazing moment when they are in the stand watching their team, as a striker puts a goal in. Or it is the feeling of salsa dancing, or the joy of listening to a certain type of music. For others, it is the buzz they get after a really good workout.

Right now, write down a time that you felt really great.

....

....

Right now, circle how strong the feeling was on a scale of 0 to 10 where 0 is very weak and 10 is very strong.

0   1   2   3   4   5   6   7   8   9   10

Right now, write down what you see when you remember the situation that makes you feel really, really great.

....

....

Right now, write down what you hear when you remember the situation that makes you feel really, really great.

....

....

Right now, write down the details of what you feel when you remember the situation that makes you feel really, really great.

....

....

We now have the first tool to start zapping rejection: this fantastic memory. It is interesting that when you remember something vividly, your brain actually starts to react physically and mentally to that memory. Think back to a delicious meal that you have eaten – you will have a physical reaction.

Remember exactly what it looked like, then take a big sniff and remember what it smelt like. Remember taking a bite and savouring the flavour and how delicious it tasted. Chances are your mouth is now watering – a physical reaction to your memory. This is a perfectly natural process that happens all the time. You can take the details from a positive memory like that, and like the one that you have been writing about, and use them to zap, or re-arrange memories you have about negative things.

Exercise

Right now, remember a time when you were rejected. It can be in a relationship situation or perhaps a work situation. It is really important that it is quite a *small* incident of rejection. On a scale of 0 to 10, it should ideally be about 3 or 4, where 0 is not rejected at all, and 10 is totally rejected. It should be about half of the score of your really fantastic feeling above. So, if you had a situation where you felt fantastic at a 10, you can go for a situation where you were rejected at a 5. Or if you have a fantastic situation at an 8 go for a 4. This is important – when you are zapping two memories it is the most powerful one that will 'win'. The bigger the difference between the two memories, the bigger the effect.

Right now, remember the time where you were rejected at a 5 or below, and write down some of the details about that situation.

....

....

Right now, circle how strong the rejection is in the memory on a scale of 0 to 10. This is your old rejection score.

0   1   2   3   4   5   6   7   8   9   10

Right now, play the CD and listen to track 2 – zapping rejection.

Now, after using my rejection zapper, the memory of the rejection is at:

0   1   2   3   4   5   6   7   8   9   10

You will notice that the memory of rejection has gone down the scale. Perhaps it is by only one point, or half a point, or it will go down substantially. It really depends. You can keep repeating this process over and over again to keep re-writing your memory of the rejection. If you eat delicious food over and over again, the more you eat it the more you will want to eat it.

In this case, the more you use the zapper, the more your rejection will be zapped.

Right now, listen to the zapping rejection track again.

Now, after using my rejection zapper, the memory of the rejection is at:

0   1   2   3   4   5   6   7   8   9   10

Right now, listen to the zapping rejection track again.

Now, after using my rejection zapper, the memory of the rejection is at:

0   1   2   3   4   5   6   7   8   9   10

Right now, listen once more to the zapping rejection track.

Now, after using my rejection zapper, the memory of the rejection is at:

0   1   2   3   4   5   6   7   8   9   10

Right now, listen to the zapping rejection track again

Now, after using my rejection zapper, the memory of the rejection is at:

0   1   2   3   4   5   6   7   8   9   10

Compare with this with your first rejection score on the previous page. Notice how much it has gone down.

Right now, look at the rejection memory. How does it look, sound and feel now? Write this down.

....

....

What is really interesting about using the rejection zapper is that these changes are permanent. Your brain is a really powerful tool, if you use it in the right way, it learns very, very quickly.

Case study

Ian hadn't been out on a date for 18 months. He had given up because of a series of dates that had gone seriously wrong. He had been rejected by several women in a row and, because of this, he was scared that if he put himself on the line again, he would only be rejected again. This was particularly frustrating as Ian had his eye on an attractive instructor at his local gym, but his fear of rejection held him back from talking to her.

We worked together using the rejection zapper. We zapped his series of bad experiences from past dates. Once the pain had been reduced, Ian felt much calmer about the idea of putting himself on the line again. He asked his gym instructor out. She said yes. That's the power of the rejection zapper.

In the same way as in the case study above, you can beat your feelings of rejection. You will have a shot at flirting opportunities that you might perhaps have passed up in the past. If you know that you can zap rejection, then it doesn't bother you so much anymore. If you know you can get rid of it, getting rejected isn't so bad in the first place.

In summary:

- Changes from the rejection zapper are permanent.
- Your brain is a powerful tool; used in the right way it learns very, very quickly.
- You can use the rejection zapper all the time.
- The rejection zapper will help change your perspective on a flirting situation.
- Zapping rejection gives you a shot at flirting opportunities that you would otherwise miss.

Frienditis in men

Frienditis is a common flirting complaint among men. Every woman I have spoken to understands this condition. They all have a friend who is lovely, wonderful, great to talk to – but they would never consider him to be relationship material. This, in essence, is 'frienditis'. The man has been placed in the 'friendship' box, rather than in the 'potential boyfriend' box in these women's minds. Once you are in the friendship box, it is hard to get out. You are suffering from frienditis if:

- women always think of you as a 'friend'
- you don't think that it is right to make the first move, as modern liberated women will take the lead
- you have lots of female friends.

Fortunately, it is not impossible to get out of the friendship box. More importantly, you need to learn how to stay out of the friendship box with the women you meet in the future. The solution to frienditis is quite simple: masculinity and confidence.

Men who suffer from frienditis give off the wrong sort of signals to the women they meet. It is as if they have a big sign around their neck saying 'I am a friendly, lovely guy'. Now, this is completely reasonable from a certain point of view. For decades now many men, including myself, have been taught that women need to be respected and treated equally. But this is where some men make the crucial mistake. There is a huge difference between masculinity and being a male chauvinist pig. You can respect women, admire their progress in their careers (earning more than you) and still be masculine at the same time. Masculinity is a crucial male trait that seems to have been tarred with the male chauvinist brush. A man can be sexy and confident, and still respect and treat women well.

More rarely, women also suffer from a variation of this disorder – 'mate-itis'. 'Mate' is a bit of an Australian term – though this can be just about anyone, your mates are usually the people that you hang out with at the pub watching the football. There is a certain breed of women who fit into this category. They make lots of jokes, they drink lots of beer, they love sport, they are great fun, but you would never really consider them girlfriend material. If this is your problem you need to pay particular attention to Chapter 7 and the next section, 'Mate-itis in women'.

In summary:

- Frienditis means a woman would never really consider you as relationship material.
- Men suffering frienditis are giving off the wrong sort of signals.
- You can be masculine without being a male chauvinist.
- Women love masculine men.
- Strong, powerful, independent women are usually still looking for a masculine man.

- 95 per cent of the time men still need to make the first move.
- Lovely guys can learn to stop coming last in the flirting game.

What can you do about frienditis?

Frienditis shows through your body language. What we feel and think about internally is reflected in our body language. Often it is much more powerful than we realize.

Mike was suffering from quite a bad case of frienditis. He had plenty of friends, particularly female friends. In fact, his frienditis was so acute that he had been sleeping in the same bed with one of his female friends that he fancied for over a year. And nothing had happened.

This guy was really interesting because he was smart, charming and popular. But clearly women put him straight in the friendship box. His body language was giving off a big sign saying 'friend' to every woman he met. Superficially, this is quite an attractive strategy to men. It means that you can approach women below the radar. Because they don't think of you as boyfriend material, it is easier to talk to them, easier to get close to them. The hope of men who employ this tactic is that once you are friends, you will be able to move things on to the next level. Well, sorry to be the bearer of bad news, but pretty much without exception, you won't. Yes, you hear about the cases of people who were great friends and then became lovers. In my experience, this is the exception rather than the rule. You have to remember that the first impression you give is extremely powerful.

In one study, tutors and lecturers were shown five-second clips of students they would be working with over the next term. They were then asked to rate how well they would get on with the students and how successful the students would be. At the end of the term, they were brought back, and again asked to make the same ratings after seeing, talking to and getting to know the students. The scores were almost exactly the same. Once you make a first impression, it is something that is very difficult to change. Once you make the first impression of 'friend' you are immediately put in that box, and you have to be a bit of a Houdini to successfully get out.

Consequently, the key is to give the right first impression. Often, it only takes a small change to make a big difference. For one man, doing the following exercises worked wonders. One of the girls who had previously thought of him as a 'friend' quite suddenly became his girlfriend. Other clients have seen more subtle but just as important results – a massive increase in the number of responses to their online profile from women, or much better results at speed-dating events.

In summary:

- What we feel and think is communicated in our body language.
- You can be smart, charming and popular, but it won't make any difference if women think of you as a friend.
- Once you are a 'friend', it is very hard to notch flirting up to the next level.
- Generally, people make up their minds about you in the first five seconds they meet you. Once in place, this impression sticks.
- The key to curing frienditis is to give the right first impression.

Boosting your masculinity

What we are going to do now is called 'modelling'. Modelling is about trying to understand what goes on in another person's head and then doing it yourself. By changing the way that you move and think, this changes your behaviour and the way you feel.

For example, you know that athletes train intensely physically. What you may not realize is that top athletes also train mentally. They go through a process of mental training – a runner will visualize a race, going through every step in their head, hearing, feeling and seeing the race, and seeing themselves winning. This mental process actually improves their performance, and the athletes who do both the mental and physical training really excel.

You can go through the mental process that other people use and apply it to yourself. The results will not be the same as those of an elite athlete, but you will feel subtle and important changes.

It is interesting that if you change how you are physically, this also changes how you feel and changes the body language you show. A client, Gawain went through this process. He was quite shy, and certainly needed a big boost in his masculinity. He was also suffering frienditis – women never really thought of him of anything more than friendship material. So we went through the process that you are about to try. We chose someone whom he wanted to model – this was a person who he would like to take a little bit of and 'inject' into his body language. For him, it was Pierce Brosnan. We imagined what Pierce Brosnan would look like when he was feeling masculine and confident. I asked him how he could tell that Pierce Brosnan was confident. There was a range of things: his chest was lifted and slightly puffed out, he had his thumbs tucked into his trousers, and he was talking to himself in a confident manner saying, 'I am in control and have power in this situation'.

Gawain tried this himself. Of course, he didn't turn magically into Pierce Brosnan, but because he changed his physical posture, he started to feel different. Because he was talking to himself in a different way there were other more subtle changes in his body language – his eyes looked more directly ahead, and he seemed slightly calmer. He became more masculine and confident. We turned this process into a CD that he took home and practised over and over again for a month.

The approach, of course, also worked in real life. He went along to a singles event, where he spoke at ease with a woman, thumbs hooked in his pockets, chest slightly puffed out, looking much more confident and more masculine. She certainly thought so – all her body language indicated that she was definitely interested. By trying to understand some of the things that Pierce Brosnan does, this man had taken a little injection of masculinity – which then changed the way the woman was reacting to him. She was certainly not thinking of him as friendship material!

Exercise

Right now, think of a man who is masculine and confident, someone you would like to take a little piece of. It is okay if this takes a little while. Write down his name.

....

Right now, circle how masculine and confident this person is, on a scale of 0 to 10, where 0 it not at all, and 10 is totally masculine and confident.

0   1   2   3   4   5   6   7   8   9   10

Right now, circle how masculine and confident you are, on a scale of 0 to 10, where 0 is not at all, and 10 is totally masculine and confident.

0   1   2   3   4   5   6   7   8   9   10

Right now, imagine that the person you are modelling has had a really bad day, that his confidence has been knocked, and he is at a 4. How does he look, feel and sound? What is going through his head? Write this down.

....

....

Right now, imagine that things are better. Your modelling person's confidence and masculinity are higher, at a 7. How does he look, feel and sound? What is going through his head? Write this down.

....

....

Right now, imagine your modelling person is totally confident. This is probably how you have seen him in the films or on TV, so it should be the easiest. His confidence and masculinity is at 10. What does he look like, what does he sound like, what is he feeling? Write this down.

....

....

Right now, imagine a situation where *you* would like to have some of this confidence and masculinity. Write down what it looks, sounds and feels like.

....

....

Right now, play the CD and listen to track 3 – boosting masculinity.

Now you have done the CD exercise, let's see if there has been any change.

Before I was masculine and confident at:

0   1   2   3   4   5   6   7   8   9   10

Now, after listening to the CD, I feel, look and sound masculine and confident at:

0   1   2   3   4   5   6   7   8   9   10

The difference may only be very subtle. It may have only increased by 1 point, or perhaps even half a point. For some people, the difference will be dramatic. Remember that your state of mind affects your body language. It starts to change the sign that you have around your neck. Just a small change can sometimes make a big difference.

If you suffer frienditis, listen to track 3 of the CD every day for the next month. This is your masculinity exercise programme. The change will be subtle, but it is like going to the gym – the more you exercise, the better you get and the easier it becomes. It is like filling up a fuel tank – when you do this exercise, it will put confidence fuel in your tank. As you use the CD regularly, slowly your tank will start to fill.

All you need to do is feel good for ten minutes a day for the next month. You will be pleasantly surprised by the results.

Mate-itis in women

A less common flirting disorder is, as I mentioned earlier in this chapter, mate-itis in women. The sort of women this affects are 'one of the boys'. They will drink beer with their male friends, watch sport, they are loud and sometimes domineering. They are great fun; unfortunately, most men don't think of them as relationship material.

Frequently, women who are suffering from mate-itis have effectively turned off their feminine signals. This can be for a wide variety of reasons. Perhaps they were brought up in a family with lots of older brothers, so this meant they spent a lot of time with boys. Again like men, some women find that being a 'mate' is a good, easy and non-threatening way to be able to hang around with men. You are probably suffering from mate-itis if:

- you are thought of as 'one of the boys'
- guys you hang out with always seem to go after other women
- guys you fancy just think of you as a friend.

This can be a slightly complex condition that needs to be treated on a one-to-one basis, but in some cases there is a simple cure. If you are suffering mate-itis, you are giving the signal that you are just friendship material. These signals need to be changed. The key is to become more sexy and flirtatious – a female variation on the male approach described above. This is covered in Chapter 7.

Desperitis

A further barrier to flirting is desperation. Desperation is something that people can seem to smell a mile away. If flirting is like running a race, then desperation is like running through mud. You don't get anywhere, and you end up looking unattractive.

The unfair thing about desperitis is that the more someone *needs* a relationship, the less likely they are to be able to find one. Basically, people who are needy are less attractive, and people who are desperate are extremely unattractive.

Nick is the epitome of desperitis. You can see how desperate he is to find a woman. He signs up first to every single event, he hands out cards with his contact details to every single woman he talks to, he has a kind of half-crazed 'please love me' look in his eyes. Furthermore, Nick's body language is over the top; he always leans in too close and seems too interested when he is speed-dating. When someone talks to Nick, whether a man or a woman, he has enormously dilated pupils.

Pupil dilation is a natural response to finding something or someone physically attractive (the black bit in our eyes gets bigger). It is something that babies do when they are young; it is a very clever tactic to make themselves more attractive to their parents and to the people who look after them. There has been a fascinating study where people were shown identical pictures of the same people. There was just one simple change – in one of the pictures, the size of their pupils was digitally increased. The photos with larger pupils were universally rated as substantially more attractive then the normal photos.

Poor Nick is so desperate that he is trying to be attractive to *everyone* he meets. This inevitably ends up having the opposite effect. Nick is showing his cards indiscriminately and far too quickly.

By being desperate you are giving a very strong message – I am needy – and perhaps suggesting that there is something wrong with your life that you want the other person to fix or fill. Do you remember those experiments where you put the two same ends of a magnet together and they push away from each other? This is what desperitis does – it pushes people away.

This can then become a self-reinforcing cycle. The more you push people away, the more desperate you become, and then the more you push people away. It is a downward spiral.

So how can you pull out? Let's take eating as an analogy. If you don't eat your breakfast, you get hungry at lunch. The less you eat, the more hungry you become. Emotions can be the same – they are a hunger, something that needs to be re-filled on a regular basis. Thus, one way to deal with desperation is to have what we could call an 'emotional breakfast'. This fills you up for the day, and changes the way you behave for the rest of the day. By the time lunchtime comes, you can be more relaxed about what you want to eat.

Case study

Ash was suffering a mild case of desperitis. Whenever he ended up talking to women that he found attractive, he was far too eager to please. He hadn't been in a relationship for quite some time and was really keen (desperate actually) to get back into one. This had a whole range of consequences. Because he was emotionally hungry, Ash reacted in a grabby desperate way. When he did meet women and got their phone number, he would text them immediately and phone the next day. This was a big sign that he was too keen.

Ash's desperation was putting women off. Desperation also had a fascinating impact on the way Ash thought. He would constantly worry about whether a woman was going to call back. He would worry about how long it took her to call back. When he was in this state of mind, he gave off desperate signals that he didn't even realize he was giving. His voice sounded different, he acted differently (e.g. texting or phoning too soon) and he thought differently. This gave the message that he was desperate.

In summary:

- Desperation is something people can smell a mile away.
- People who are needy are extremely unattractive.

- Being desperate sends a message that you are needy and that there is perhaps something wrong with your life.
- Desperitis can become a self-reinforcing cycle, making people more and more desperate.
- Emotions are a hunger that need to be fed on a regular basis.
- Get your emotional breakfast and you will be less hungry at lunch!
- Even if you are a great match, desperation may put someone off.
- When you are in a non-desperate state of mind, your actions will be completely different.

What can you do about desperitis?

So what is the solution? I gave Ash his emotional breakfast. I asked him to remember back to a time when he was in a happy relationship, a time when he felt really content and happy, the opposite of desperate. For him, it was a particular moment when he was driving with his girlfriend on a holiday in the USA. There they were in the car, with the freedom of the road, he had his fantastic girlfriend beside him, and he felt on top of the world.

I asked him to describe this to me again in detail. I asked him to remember how it looked, sounded and felt. When you remember something really vividly, the feelings that you had at the time start to come back and it has a physical impact.

By just thinking about a situation in the past, you start to bring back strong emotions. Ash revisited emotions and thoughts from a time when he felt content, when he felt satisfied, when he had his emotional breakfast. He then visualized this time intensely, spending some time sitting in the emotions, sights and sounds. His state of mind changed.

Then, when he thought about getting a phone number from a girl and how quickly he would call, the situation was entirely different. 'I'll call her when I have time', 'I'm not really fussed'. By having his emotional breakfast, Ash had gone from being desperate to content.

Breakfast is something you need every day. The same goes for an emotional breakfast. If you stop, you will become hungry again. By being a little bit less desperate though, you are removing the desperation brake on your flirting. This will allow you to get what you really want. You will notice that people start to react to you more positively, which in turn makes you feel less desperate. And then this becomes a positive self-inforcing cycle. The less desperate you are, the better people will react to you, which will make you less desperate. Then you start getting your breakfast from the people around you.

Exercise

Right now, write down a situation, where, like Ash, you felt emotionally full. It could be a past relationship, or a time with friends and family.

....

....

Right now, remember the situation in detail. Write down the things that you saw, looking from your own eyes.

....

....

Right now, remember the sounds and conversations of the situation. Write down what you heard.

....

....

Right now, remember how good it felt being in this situation, how good it felt being emotionally satisfied. Write down how you felt.

....

....

Right now, think of a situation where you felt desperate. Look at it from the outside. Write down what it was like, and what you were thinking.

....

....

Right now, write down the three best things that are happening in your life. Picture them.

1

2

3

Right now, play the CD and listen to track 4 – emotional breakfast.

Remember that, just like breakfast, getting your emotional breakfast is something you need to do every day. Listen to track 4 every day – it will only take a short amount of time and will make a huge difference to your flirting. The more you use it, the more you will top up your emotional fuel tank. Once you start getting your breakfast from being in a relationship, you replace the CD with a real person!

Stranger danger

As a rule, in big cities, you never chat to people on public transport and you rarely chat with people in the shops. When you do try and chat to people, they shy away, presuming that you might want something. On going home at night, people look suspiciously at each other, thinking they may get mugged.

What has this got to do with flirting? It's actually a huge flirting brake that some people suffer from – stranger danger. We are told as children that we shouldn't talk to strangers, but the statistical reality is that children are rarely attacked by strangers, they are more likely to suffer at the hands of their friends and family. People may carry this mentality of 'stranger danger' into their adult life, especially if they are living in a big city.

In essence, the stranger danger approach is the polar opposite to flirting. Flirting is about being open, about being friendly, about having interactions with people that are fun just for the sake of it. Flirting is about meeting and connecting with new people and not expecting anything from them, except perhaps a little fun, flirtatious conversation. The attitude of stranger danger means that we are suspicious of meeting new people. We are closed to making connections and having fun interactions with people. With flirting, if you have the stranger danger attitude, you are missing out on flirting opportunities all the time.

I have to add that there is of course an element of truth in the issue of stranger danger – of course you need to be on guard when appropriate. If someone approaches you in a dark alley, obviously you shouldn't have a flirty conversation with them! The context in which you meet a stranger is important to bear in mind. The key is to treat people as innocent until proven guilty; 99 per cent of people are good friendly people. It is a case of being open to them, while keeping an eye out for that 1 per cent who could cause you trouble.

Quite a stark example of how I could have missed out through stranger danger is the story of how I met my partner.

I was out with one of my clients on a Saturday night. She was a very quick student – keen and a fast learner. By 9 p.m. she had already met a man and had been chatting with him for some time. I had been chatting to his friend who otherwise would have been left out of the conversation. My client pulled me aside, leant over and whispered in my ear, 'We're going back to my place, you can take the rest of the night off'. Result!

It was a Saturday night and I had been planning to spend the whole evening out with my client 'practising'. There was no way that I was going home early – there was the rest of the night before me! I continued to chat to the friend of the guy who my client took home – it turned out that he was there with a whole bunch of other people. At this point, they were just going to another bar. I had to make a decision: go with this bunch of strangers to another bar or go home.

Well, we wandered down the street to another bar – played some pool, drank some beer. I was flirting with one of the women in the group who seemed pretty keen, the night was looking like it was going to be fun. I decided that I should go and cruise the bar and look for flirting signals. In retrospect, I realize that I was going to do my shopping, checking out everything that was available and taking the pick of the ones that I liked best. I excused myself from my newly-found friends and wandered through the bar. On the dance floor, a gorgeous woman caught my eye – she looked up and gave me a big bright green light. She immediately struck me because of her dancing and her clothes. I have a thing about the way someone dances, I find that the way someone moves reflects their personality and attitude to life. I moved straight in for the kill and the rest is history. We now live together in our lovely renovated house in east London.

Who would have thought that I would have met the love of my life in a pool bar? If I had been suffering from stranger danger, I would have never made it to that bar. I would have never met the woman who brings such love and happiness into my life.

Stranger danger is a cultural and regional issue. In my experience, Londoners suffer terribly from stranger danger. People in small town England don't. Most Americans that I have met don't seem to suffer from stranger danger, they are friendly with just about every one that they meet.

You are suffering from stranger danger if:

• you are suspicious of the new people that you meet
• you rarely chat to new people just for the fun of it
• you think that everyone must want something from you if they start up a conversation.

What can you do about stranger danger?

Now we have established the dangers of stranger danger, what can you do about it? You are going to focus on some of the positive memories you have of when you are really open to people, and cut and paste them to a situation where you have unreasonably suffered from stranger danger. This process will start to programme your brain to be more open to meeting people, while at the same time keeping in place all the safety guards that you need.

Exercise

Right now, write down a situation where you have suffered stranger danger where, in retrospect, you realize you could have been more open to that person.

....

....

Right now, write down what you saw, heard and how you felt.

....

....

Right now, circle how strong your feeling of stranger danger is on a scale of 0 to 10, where 0 is no stranger danger and 10 is total stranger danger.

0   1   2   3   4   5   6   7   8   9   10

Right now, think of a situation where you were really open to the people around you and you were having a brilliant time – for instance, a friend's birthday party or on a holiday with friends.

Right now, remember what the situation looked like and write it down.

....

....

Right now, remember what the situation felt like and write it down.

....

....

Right now, remember what the open situation sounded like and write it down.

....

....

Right now, play the CD and listen to track 5 – stranger danger.

When you have finished listening to the track, again remember the 'stranger danger situation'. How does it look and feel now?

Right now, circle how strong your feeling of stranger danger is on a scale of 0 to 10, where 0 is no stranger danger and 10 is total stranger danger.

0   1   2   3   4   5   6   7   8   9   10

Right now, listen to track 5 again. When you have finished listening to the track, remember the 'stranger danger situation' again. How does it look and feel now?

Right now, circle how strong your feeling of stranger danger is on a scale of 0 to 10, where 0 is no stranger danger and 10 is total stranger danger.

0   1   2   3   4   5   6   7   8   9   10

Right now, listen once more to track 5. When you have finished listening to the track, remember the 'stranger danger situation' again. How does it look and feel now?

Right now, circle how strong your feeling of stranger danger is on a scale of 0 to 10, where 0 is no stranger danger and 10 is total stranger danger.

0   1   2   3   4   5   6   7   8   9   10

Right now, listen again to track 5. When you have finished listening to the track, remember the 'stranger danger situation' again. How does it look and feel now?

Right now, circle how strong your feeling of stranger danger is on a scale of 0 to 10, where 0 is no stranger danger and 10 is total stranger danger.

0   1   2   3   4   5   6   7   8   9   10

How does this compare with the score when you started the exercise? Notice how much the stranger danger has reduced.

Right now, think about the stranger danger situation again. How does it look, sound and feel now? Write this down.

....

....

You should be able to see that using this method, piece by piece, reduces your stranger danger. Keep chipping away at it until your stranger danger is down to a 1 or 2.

This is not a miracle cure for stranger danger – it is more a way of opening your mind to the idea of meeting new people. Once you hear, feel and see that your stranger danger has been reduced, you will notice that your actions start to change when put in the situation. It may only be a small difference, but sometimes that small difference can be enough. Perhaps rather than standing in silence at the bus stop next to the person who looks quite interesting, you will start a conversation about how the bus is running late. When you visit the local store, maybe you will have a chat with the person serving you. Once you start making these little steps, you will realize that the people around you are just that: people. This becomes a self-reinforcing cycle. Little by little you can shift your stranger danger – you never know, a great friend, the love or your life or just a fun conversation could be standing right next to you.

In summary:

- Stranger danger puts a huge brake on flirting.
- A new great friend or the love of your life could be a 'stranger'.
- It is possible to reduce your stranger danger to allow you to be more open and flirtatious.

Bastarditis and bitchitis

Bastard and bitchitis are other forms of flirting disorders that will hold back your flirting skills. Essentially, they are the situations where you are attracted to the wrong sort of person. Often, the most attractive women you encounter at singles nights suffer from bastarditis. They complain about how bad their last relationship was, tell you how badly they were treated and how it is so hard to find a good man. Of course, there are plenty of nice looking men for them – ones who will treat them well. Point one out, however, and immediately their response is 'No, he looks too nice, I'm not attracted to him'. It is that old cliché of being attracted to the dark horse. The bad guy. The one you know is going to be trouble.

Men can also suffer from bitchitis. John, for example, went through a series of relationships where he was attracted to ice queens over and over again. The more he wanted to get close to them, the further they moved away. The more he wanted them to be available, the less available they were. The problem was that when he saw these sorts of women, it was as if a light went on over their heads – they were surrounded by this attractive glow that couldn't be resisted. He was like a moth flying into a fire – he knew he was going to get burnt, but he went anyway.

His friends just couldn't understand this pattern. 'But John, you are such a warm, friendly and open person. How could you end up with an ice queen?'

We have a 'relationship template' that outlines who we are attracted to. There is a series of things experienced in past relationships that somehow press our buttons. If you really understand body language, you realize that you can read an enormous amount about a person in the first few seconds that you meet. You can see if they are energetic or depressed. You can gauge if you are going to get on with them. Normally, when you meet someone, your mind matches their body language and facial features against the database of people that you have met in the past. If they match up with your 'relationship template', then you experience that chemistry.

With John, it was as if he was wearing a pair of special glasses – every time he saw an ice queen, they lit up with that attractive glow. He needed a new pair of glasses so that when he saw a better type of woman, she would light up with an attractive glow. Or at least the ice queens would lose their shine.

I worked with John to change his relationship glasses. He is now in a relationship with a lovely, warm and available woman: the complete opposite of an ice queen.

One of my other clients also suffered from quite a nasty case of bastarditis. She was attracted to men that she had to save and who were unavailable. Whenever she needed them they were never around – and they particularly didn't have any time for her because they were focused on their careers. There was not much use working on her flirting skills, if she was going to keep on picking bad eggs. Therefore, I used this process of cleaning up her relationship glasses. Since then she has met a lovely, available man. The profession that he has chosen to follow gives him plenty of spare time for her and their family. One of the first things that she was amazed by and that we discussed was just how available he was. They are now married.

This technique is complex and unfortunately it is beyond the scope of this book. It is personally tailored – each case is different.

You suffer from bastarditis if:

- you are always attracted to the wrong sort of man
- men who would be good for you don't seem attractive
- you repeat the same patterns over and over again.

You are suffering from bitchitis if:

- you are always attracted to the wrong sort of woman
- women who would be great for you don't seem attractive
- you repeat the same bad patterns over and over again.

In summary:

- You suffer from bastard or bitchitis if you are continually attracted to the wrong sort of person.
- We have a relationship template of the type of person that we are attracted to.
- It is possible to change your relationship template.

Gender confusion disorder – who does what?

During the 2000s there have been huge changes in the dating and flirting scene. People who have come out of a long-term relationship have said to me that it is a little like stepping out of a time machine into a completely new world. Internet dating is now huge, speed-dating is commonplace, there is a whole new *Sex in the City* generation of women who have grown up with powerful and different dating role models.

What you might have found, and certainly what many of my clients find, is that, because of this, there is a lot of confusion about gender roles and what the new rules are. Who asks for the phone number? Who suggests the next date? Who makes the first move? Men don't know if they should make the first move; women aren't sure if they should be more assertive. I call this 'gender confusion disorder'.

You need to know that although we are living in the twenty-first century, effectively the rules for flirting have very much stayed in the twentieth century.

Who does what? What are the new rules? A useful way to think about it is to imagine that flirting is like a puppet show. The woman takes the role of the puppeteer and the man the role of the puppet. If you are watching them, it seems like the man is taking all the action. But in reality, it is the woman who is guiding and controlling what the man is doing – he is simply responding to her decisions. It is exactly the same with flirting, and many people seem to forget this.

If you are the woman, you need to guide the direction in which you want the flirting to go. If you are a man, you need to respond to the woman's guidance by taking action.

Case study

Meeta is in her mid 40s and suffers from gender confusion disorder. This was highlighted in her approach to internet dating. She is successful, outgoing, bubbly and quite forceful. Her approach online was to take the action role of the man. She would send out quite long emails to the men that she fancied, being really forward and taking the lead. She dismissed the idea that she should take the traditional flirting role of making it clear that she was interested and then letting the man do the work. When we first started working together, no men approached her, and she was getting a zero response rate to her email. Meeta was being the puppet rather than the puppeteer.

I worked with her to change her tactics so that they fitted much more with the traditional flirting role. We toned down her profile and got her to take on the puppeteer's role – she searched through men's profiles, picked the ones that she liked and then sent them a 'wink' – this was just a short email indicating that she liked their profile and was interested in them getting in touch. Almost immediately there was a dramatic turnaround in her success rate. Meeta got more replies than she had ever had before, and even got some unsolicited approaches from men who liked her profile. She is now successfully going out on dates.

Key points for you if you are a woman:

- We live in the twenty-first century, but generally gender roles are the same as in the twentieth century.
- If in doubt, take the traditional flirting role.
- Make it clear that you are interested.
- Let the man take action.
- Remember that men may be intimidated by a direct approach.
- Play the puppeteer, not the puppet.

Case study

Matt was suffering the male version of gender confusion disorder. He posted his profile on a dating website and waited for the women to come to him. He had been on the website for seven months and had not had any dates. He was failing to take up the man's traditional flirting role, which is that of the hunter. It is the man's role to spot the signals that a woman is interested in him and then to take action.

I worked with him to change his approach so that he looked through online profiles, carefully picked the women that he was interested in, and made sure that he strongly fitted their criteria. He then sent them thoughtful emails, based on the information he had read in their profiles. He switched his role from being passive, to the traditional role of the active man. The results were brilliant – Matt had a 45 per cent response rate to his emails – and he arranged a whole bunch of dates. Within a week, he had stopped sending out emails because he wanted to concentrate on the dates that he had arranged!

Key points if you are a man:

- You are the puppet – you need to respond to the puppeteer's orders!
- It is up to you to take action – either look for a flirting green light or on dating websites make sure that you fit the criteria and then take action.
- If in doubt, take the traditional male role.

The gender rules for flirting are quite simple. The woman picks the man she is interested in and makes it clear that she is available. She guides the action – from first giving eye contact, to hinting that she would like to go out for a drink some time. It is the man's job to take action, watch out for the signals and act by starting a conversation with a women who gives a flirting green light. He should ask for her phone number when she hints it might be fun to catch up for a drink, give her a call and arrange the next date. If in doubt, stick to tradition.

I must end on a caveat. Flirting and dating rules are changing, but very slowly. It is fine for a woman to make the first move but you have to realize that if you break the traditional flirting rules there is the danger that things won't go to plan. If you are confident in approaching men, getting their phone numbers etc., good for you, but you need to stick to the task with gusto. If you take that role, stick to it! Don't expect the man to suddenly start chasing you!

Successitis

As women become more and more successful in their careers, they may begin to suffer from successitis. Successitis can put a major brake on flirting. A useful way to think about successitis is that it makes you look like you have a suit of armour on. You seem invulnerable, strong, tough and independent.

Case study

Lavina and Meryl both suffered from quite bad cases of successitis. They are both models and are very successful in what they do. They earn a lot of money, travel frequently, and of course are very attractive. Their problem was that they couldn't find decent boyfriends. At first, this seems quite amazing. They were gorgeous models, they had money, they had time; great men should be flocking to them. What they found was that the men that they liked never approached them. The only types of men who did approach them were the super overconfident types.

It seems they had developed a type of armour plating. Initially, because they were both so attractive, they had been approached by men all the time. If they gave off the slightest flirting signal in public, then men would approach them. Quite reasonably, being sick of this, they learned to completely turn off their flirting signals, without really realizing it. It was as if they were walking around with their flirting signalling system permanently on red. The only type of men who would approach them were the ones who were willing to run red lights; the men they fancied saw the red lights and didn't approach, and were extra intimidated by their good looks.

Instead, Lavina and Meryl learned to give green lights to the men they fancied by making eye contact. They learned that they had to make it really, really easy for the guys that they fancied to approach them. Essentially, because they were so attractive and successful, their flirting signals had to be three times as bright. And it worked a treat.

Some women, who work in a male-dominated corporate environment, have to learn to turn their flirting signals off as well. Generally, the corporate environment is a very masculine and competitive place. Being feminine and flirtatious is often frowned upon. Office romances can be risky for your career and so many women take a preventative approach by making sure that they don't flirt with anyone in the workplace. These sorts of women develop a kind of 'work armour' to protect them. Their flirting signalling system also becomes jammed on red. They then carry this 'corporate armour' into their personal lives. They seem terribly business-like and confident. But not in the least flirtatious.

As a woman, you may be suffering from successitis if:

- the only men who approach you are overconfident or bastards
- the men you do like never talk to you
- men seem intimidated by you
- you are told that you seem unavailable – even though you may feel otherwise
- you find it hard to switch from work mode to flirt mode.

Very few men suffer from successitis. Women generally don't seem to be intimidated by men who are more successful or more powerful than them. In fact, many studies show that women actively seek out men who are of a higher status and income than themselves – scientists speculate that this is because they would make better providers for the women's children. (See SIRC Guide to Flirting, *What social science can tell you about flirting and how to do it*, Kate Fox, SIRC, 1999.)

If you are suffering from successitis, what can you do about it? You have to learn to take off your armour around the men that you fancy:

- Learn how to give green lights to men that you fancy – see Chapter 5.
- Give stronger green lights than normal – you may need to give several green lights to get a man to approach you. You may need to make it very easy for him to approach or contact you.
- Seem more feminine and approachable – see Chapter 7.

Shrinking violet syndrome

Shrinking violet syndrome is another common ailment that can hold your flirting back. Essentially, this means you are shy. There are two versions of this syndrome – the introvert and the extrovert shrinking violet. In general, people are either very obviously shy, or they are extremely extroverted but really shy on the inside.

One of the most common versions of the shrinking violet syndrome is someone who is very confident at work, but completely loses their confidence when faced with a dating situation.

Tom is a surgeon. He is incredibly confident in his work – he has to save lives almost every day. He described a situation where he was on a ward – from the corner of his eye he spotted a patient's heart monitor that was looking strange. He walked over to the patient, explained that he had an irregular heartbeat and that he might be about to go into cardiac arrest. As he was speaking, the patient suddenly started having a heart attack. The patient's family became hysterical – they thought they were watching their beloved father and husband dying. Tom was calm. He called the nurses, attached the equipment, checked the charge levels, called 'clear' and brought the man back to life. In the sort of situation that would terrify most, he was calm and confident.

When it comes to dating, Tom is the exact opposite. Faced with a woman, suddenly he becomes clammy and uncomfortable. He doesn't know what to say. He feels he doesn't know how to flirt and cannot see the signs if they are interested. He is suffering from the extrovert version of the shrinking violet syndrome – if you met him in his career and everyday life, you would never guess it.

Krishnan, however, is just plain shy. He is the one at every singles event sitting in the corner nursing his drink. He would never approach a woman to start a conversation. And yet he is a lovely man. He will make some woman a great husband or boyfriend; he is just too shy to be able to show that off.

Do you recognize any of these symptoms? You suffer from shrinking violet syndrome if:

- you tend to hide in the corner at events and parties
- you are externally confident but when you speak to people that you actually find attractive, suddenly you become shy
- you stumble over conversation when talking to people that you find attractive.

The trouble with shrinking violet syndrome is that it strikes at the heart of your flirting skills – you have to be confident enough to actually give flirting signals. Shrinking violets are often so shy that they can't.

So what can you do about it? The simplest solution is to cut and paste the confident feelings, thoughts, sights and sounds you have from another experience on to situations where you are currently a shrinking violet. This is a gradual process, but the key is to start increasing your confidence in flirting situations.

Sue is a merchant banker. She deals with millions in currency every single day, but she suffered from shrinking violet syndrome. At singles events she was happy to talk to other women, but terrified of starting conversations with the men that she found attractive. She took confidence from another part of her life – work – and cut and pasted it onto social situations. Of course, it is not possible to become as totally confident at flirting as you are at work in a few moments, but she took some of her work-related confidence and transferred it to a flirting situation.

At the next event Sue attended, she found herself circulating, chatting to men she fancied. She still seemed quite shy, but by taking some of the confidence from her work, she had managed to push through the shrinking violet barrier and got off the starting plate.

Tom the surgeon did the same. He actually used the confidence that he had in the situation where he was saving a patient's life – he remembered exactly what it looked, sounded and felt like. He captured that feeling and then pasted into the context of going speed-dating. In the past with speed-dating, he struggled to hold a decent conversation and felt he didn't know what to say.

Now, using the confidence he had in his work, his whole approach was different. He felt more in control, more relaxed, more assured that there would be some sort of positive outcome and not really worrying if there wasn't. The results were very impressive. Before he would only get one or two ticks when speed-dating, he now regularly gets 11 or 12: a massive improvement in anyone's books!

The key to being a shrinking violet is your state of mind. If you are feeling shy, that will be reflected in the way that you look and sound. People will see you, and their first impression will be 'shy'. Contrast this with your state of mind when you are in a situation where you are confident. Think back to reactions that people have given you – they treat you as if you are a confident person. The situation where you are confident could be at work, it could be playing chess, it could be playing pool, or it could be cooking.

Exercise

You are now going to take some of your confidence from another area of your life and cut and paste a little bit of it onto your shy approach to dating.

Right now, write down the thing that you are at your most confident when doing. It can be anything; work, playing video games, sport, getting bargains at sales, running etc.

....

Right now, remember a specific time when you were doing what you are really confident about. It needs to be a time when you were feeling really confident, as close to 10 as possible, where 10 is totally confident, and 0 is not confident at all. Write it down.

....

....

Right now, remember what the confident situation looked like – write down all the visual details that you can remember.

....

....

Right now, remember what the confident situation sounded like – write down the conversations and sounds.

....

....

Right now, remember what the confident situation felt like – write down the sensations and confident feelings.

....

....

Right now, circle how confident you were in the confident situation on a scale of 0 to 10, where 0 is not confident at all and 10 is totally confident.

0   1   2   3   4   5   6   7   8   9   10

Right now, remember a flirting situation where you were being a shrinking violet. Write down a short description of the situation from start to finish.

....

....

Right now, circle how confident you felt in that shrinking violet situation on a scale of 0 to 10, where 0 is not confident at all and 10 is totally confident.

0   1   2   3   4   5   6   7   8   9   10

Right now, play the CD and listen to track 6 – shrinking violet syndrome.

Right now, look over the shrinking violet flirting situation in your head, listen to the sounds and take note of the feelings. Circle how confident are you about the situation on a scale of 0 to 10, where 0 is not confident at all and 10 is totally confident.

0   1   2   3   4   5   6   7   8   9   10

Right now, listen to track 6 again. Look over the shrinking violet flirting situation in your head, listen to the sounds and take note of the feelings. Circle how confident are you about the situation on a scale of 0 to 10, where 0 is not confident at all and 10 is totally confident.

0   1   2   3   4 . 5   6   7   8   9   10

Right now, listen once more to track 6. Look over the shrinking violet flirting situation in your head, listen to the sounds and take note of the feelings. Circle how confident are you about the situation on a scale of 0 to 10, where 0 is not confident at all and 10 is totally confident.

0   1   2   3   4   5   6   7   8   9   10

Right now, listen again to track 6. Look over the shrinking violet flirting situation in your head, listen to the sounds and take note of the feelings. Circle how confident are you about the situation on a scale of 0 to 10, where 0 is not confident at all and 10 is totally confident.

0   1   2   3   4   5   6   7   8   9   10

Right now, circle your first shrinking violet score (see opposite) in the flirting situation and compare this with your last score above.

0   1   2   3   4   5   6   7   8   9   10

Right now, think about the shrinking violet situation again. How does it look, sound and feel now? Write this down.

....

....

Compare the two scores above and what you have written. How much have they changed? It may only be a little, it may be a lot, but sometimes a small shift is enough to get you taking action.

Jan is a bit of a shrinking violet. Her issue was that she was too shy to give eye contact to the men she fancied so she was never approached by the men she was attracted to. At the start of this exact same exercise, Jan's confidence score was 3. By the end of it, she had reached a 5. This made all the difference. At the start of the session, she was saying that there was no way that she could give eye contact because she felt so shy. By the time she hit 5, her attitude was completely different – she walked out of the room willing to give it a try. If you can do it in your head, then you are 90 per cent of the way to being able to do it in real life.

If you are shy, keep listening to the CD over and over until your confidence has reached a stage where you feel more comfortable about starting to take some action.

When you are faced with a situation where you might need some more confidence, you can imagine this situation while you are using the CD. The surgeon, Tom, imagined that he was going out speed-dating – which was the situation where he needed more confidence. He then used his CD to cut and paste the feelings of confidence onto that situation. The merchant banker, Sue, imagined that she was going to a singles event and talking with both men and women. She then used the CD to cut and paste her confidence onto that situation.

In summary:

- Shrinking violet syndrome holds back your ability to flirt – you can't flirt if you are too shy to do it in the first place!
- You suffer from shrinking violet syndrome if you tend to hide in the corner at events and parties or you are externally confident, but really shy underneath.
- If you are in a shy state of mind, people can read this from your body language and voice tone.
- When you are in a confident state of mind, people will see, hear and feel this in your body language.
- Your mind can be pre-programmed to cut and paste the confidence that you have in one situation onto your flirting.
- Think about situations where you would like to be more confident and then use them in the CD.

05

flirting – introduction to the basic rules

In this chapter you will learn:
- about the flirting traffic signals, and the importance of red and green lights
- as a woman, how to give green signals
- as a man, spotting the green signals.

Now that we have covered the things that might be holding back your flirting, we can move forward. The first step in flirting is to really understand and practise the most basic rules. This chapter explains the ABC of flirting. I recommend that you go through it carefully, though it may seem basic, because it is crucial to get this right.

For most people flirting, the basics is where they are going wrong. If you have just one of the flirting puzzle pieces missing, then you will fall flat on your face.

Flirting traffic signals

Flirting is a mating ritual between the different members of our species. As with all rituals, there is a series of signals and moves that each person in the ritual makes. It is like a dance between two partners and it is vital to understand the most basic steps.

Over the years, explaining the flirting dance, I have found that the easiest way to describe the whole process is to use the analogy of traffic signals. When you are driving, traffic signals are clear, unambiguous signals telling you what action you need to take on the road. When you see a red light, you stop. When you see a green light, you go. Everyone understands these rules and, as a result, many people can travel on our roads every day. When people break the rules, then you get trouble: traffic accidents that can be costly and dangerous. When you boil flirting down to the basics, there is also a set of clear basic signals that govern the most basic steps in the flirting dance:

- Women select their potential mate.
- The woman gives the man a green light.
- The man has to take action.
- If a woman is not interested, she will give a red light.

This process is repeated over and over again during the dance of flirting. Women essentially lead the way, give the signals for the direction to be taken, and then the men take the action.

When you understand this most basic of processes, it makes what seems like a complicated and difficult process very simple. You need to learn how to either give the right sort of signals, or read the signals and take action. In this way, flirting is like learning to drive: think of this book as your highway code!

Women give their green light signals through a series of simple ritualized body language and verbal signals. There is a signal when they show initial interest, a signal when they fancy the man, and signals for when they would like to take the man home! Once you start to understand these signals, the process of flirting becomes as easy as watching traffic signals on the road.

Women – giving the green light

The first and most important signal that a woman can give is the green light. It is the most important signal because it starts the whole flirting process moving. Without a green light, men don't know what to do and women don't end up getting the men that they want.

If you are a woman, turning on your green light is terribly simple. Look around, select the man you fancy and make eye contact with him. Then repeat.

The trick to giving a green light is to get the timing just right. Eye contact is an extremely powerful body language signal. Psychologists have found that you can tell whether new couples are in love by how much time they spend looking into each other's eyes. If there is eye contact more than 70 per cent of the time, then chances are they are in love.

In many books on flirting you will learn how important eye contact is. However, they may not spend time explaining how completely crucial the *timing* of your eye contact is. Talking to many of my clients, they understand that eye contact is critical, but they don't really understand, or feel comfortable, with how long it should last. Men are confused about how long indicates a green light, and women are concerned that if they look for too long they will seem desperate.

Most flirting books tell you that a woman needs to maintain eye contact for three seconds or more. How do you actually do this in real life? How do you manage to get the timing just right? Because eye contact is such an intense experience and most people realize what a strong and important message it is sending, giving eye contact can seem to last a lot longer than it actually does. Typically, a woman can make eye contact with a man and say that it 'felt like ages', while the man would say that it 'didn't last long at all'.

You need a tool to get the timing exactly right. The following simple rules for women work best:

- Catch the man's eye.
- In your head slowly say, 'You are really gorgeous'.
- Look away.
- Look back, catch the man's eye, smile.
- In your head slowly say, 'You are really gorgeous'.
- Look away again.

If 'gorgeous' doesn't work for you, substitute another word, for instance:

- 'You are really sexy.'
- 'You are really hot.'
- 'You are really fit.'

It is important that you say the entire sentence. All four words. This makes the timing of your green signal just long enough so that a man can spot it, and just short enough so that you don't seem desperate.

Practising your green light

When working on a one-to-one basis with my female clients, I normally take their green lights through a three-stage process. First, I get them to practise on me – this feels safe as we are in a nice private office, or perhaps at a singles event where we have been chatting for some time. Once they are comfortable with this first stage, we move on to the second stage of dummy runs. I get them to practise on guys that they don't really fancy, but that they wouldn't mind talking to. Think of it as trying on a dress that you don't really want to buy, just for fun. The third stage is practising on guys that they really like. For each of my clients, progression depends on how comfortable they are with the eye contact.

When working with my clients at each stage, if they are feeling uncomfortable, we use a similar process to the one on the CD that comes with this book. We cut and paste feelings, sights and sounds from a situation they feel comfortable with onto the situation of giving a green light.

So, are you ready? Now we are going to do the same.

Exercise

Stage 1 – book practice

The first stage is for you to practise in a nice safe environment. What better environment than this book?

Right now, look at the picture below. Look into the man's eyes and say in your head, 'You are really gorgeous'. Then look away again. Look back, smile, and say, 'You are really gorgeous'. Then look away again.

Photo 3

Right now, circle how comfortable you are with giving the man in the photo eye contact on a scale of 0 to 10, where 0 is not comfortable at all, and 10 is totally comfortable.

0   1   2   3   4   5   6   7   8   9   10

What is your score? If you score is less than 8, then carry on with this exercise. If you score an 8 or more, skip to stage 2 – window shopping.

Right now, think of something that makes you feel fantastic; really, really excited. For some people this can be dancing, eating chocolate, bungee jumping, or walking in the mountains. Now I want you to think of something that makes you feel the most excited you can remember. On a scale of 0 to 10, where 0 is nothing and 10 is the most amazing you can ever remember feeling, it must be as close to 10 as possible. Sometimes people can only think of a 5 or an 8. That is okay too, but it must be the highest, best memory that you can remember right now.

Right now, write down the thing that makes you feel amazing.

....

....

Right now, write down the specific time when you were doing this thing that made you feel amazing.

....

....

Right now, remember the specific time that made you feel really, really excited and write down what you saw, through your own eyes.

....

....

Right now, remember the specific time that made you feel amazing and write down what you heard with your own ears.

....

....

Right now, remember the specific time that made you feel amazing and write down how you felt, the sensations you had inside your body.

....

....

Right now, play the CD and listen to track 7 – practicing your green light.

Right now, look at the picture opposite. Look into the man's eyes and say in your head, 'You are really gorgeous'. Then look away again. Look back, smile, and say, 'You are really gorgeous', and then look away again.

Photo 4

Right now, circle how comfortable you are with giving the man in the photo eye contact on a scale of 0 to 10, where 0 is not comfortable at all, and 10 is totally comfortable.

0   1   2   3   4   5   6   7   8   9   10

What is your score? If it is an 8 or more, move on to stage 2 – window shopping. If your score is 7 or below, right now play track 7 again. Keep repeating this process until you have a score of at least 8. You might need to listen to the CD (track 7) four or five times to get you to the right level. Then move on to stage 2 – window shopping.

This process is starting to re-programme your mind to be more comfortable with the first stage of giving green lights.

Stage 2 – window shopping

Stage 2 involves giving green lights to men that you don't really fancy but that you would be happy to talk to. It is a little like going window shopping or trying on a dress that you don't really intend to buy. Practising on someone you don't really fancy is much easier than going for someone you do fancy. You will find that there is less at stake. People are more comfortable giving a green light to someone they don't really fancy at first. As the old saying goes 'You need to walk before you can run'!

If you are not in a public place, then take this book somewhere public. Go out for a coffee. Sit in a park. Go to a gallery. Go for lunch or just look out the window. If you are reading at home, well, you need to do this exercise tomorrow and write down the results.

Right now, have a look around you using your peripheral vision and see if you can spot any guys who fit into the 'window shopping' category. We are talking about someone who you wouldn't mind if they asked you for directions.

Right now, pick the window shopping guy. Use your peripheral vision to keep an eye on which direction he is looking in. When he looks towards you, hold eye contact and say in your head 'I am window shopping'. Look back down. Repeat, hold eye contact and say in your head, 'I am window shopping'. Look back down.

Right now, circle how comfortable you are window shopping on a scale of 0 to 10, where 0 is totally uncomfortable, and 10 is totally comfortable.

0   1   2   3   4   5   6   7   8   9   10

If your score is 8 or more, skip to stage 3 – people you actually fancy.

If your score is below 8, then **right now play the CD and listen to track 7 again.**

What is your score now? If it is still below 8, keep repeating the track until you reach a score of 8.

0   1   2   3   4   5   6   7   8   9   10

Window shop until you are comfortable

Now you are more comfortable with window shopping in your head, it's time to try it in real life again.

Right now, have a look around you using your peripheral vision and see if you can spot any guys who fit into the 'window shopping' category.

Right now, pick the window shopping guy. Use your peripheral vision to keep an eye on which direction he is looking in. When he looks towards you, hold eye contact and say in your head, 'I am window shopping'. Look back down. Repeat, hold eye contact and say in your head, 'I am window shopping'. Look back down.

Right now, circle how comfortable you are doing this on a scale of 0 to 10, where 0 is totally uncomfortable and 10 is totally comfortable.

0   1   2   3   4   5   6   7   8   9   10

If your score is below 8, **right now play the CD and listen to track 7 again.**

What is your score now? Circle it. If it is still below 8, then listen to the CD again. Keep repeating the track until you reach a score of 8.

0   1   2   3   4   5   6   7   8   9   10

This whole process is slowly re-programming your brain to be more comfortable with giving green lights. Once you reach a score of 8, move to stage 3 – people you actually fancy.

Stage 3 – people you actually fancy!
Practising in your mind
The final stage is to practise your green lights on men that you actually fancy. You are going to start by practising on someone you have fancied in the past. This is a kind of mental dummy run for giving a green light in real life.

Right now, write down the name of a guy that you have fancied in the past.

....

Right now, imagine that he is standing in front of you. Write down how he looks.

....

....

Right now, imagine that he is standing in front of you. Write down how he sounds.

....

....

Right now, imagine that he is standing in front of you. Write down how you feel about him.

....

....

Right now, vividly imagine giving him a green light.

Look into his eyes and say to yourself in your head, 'You are really gorgeous'. Look away. Look into his eyes, smile and say, 'You are really gorgeous'. Look away.

How comfortable are you with giving him a green light on a scale of 0 to 10, where 0 is totally uncomfortable and 10 is totally comfortable?

    0   1   2   3   4   5   6   7   8   9   10

If your score is 8 or more, well done! Skip to the next section – practising in real life. If your score is 7 or less, **right now play the CD on track 7.**

Now, vividly imagine giving the person you fancy a green light.

Look into his eyes and say to yourself in your head, 'You are really gorgeous'. Look away. Look into his eyes, smile and say, 'You are really gorgeous'. Look away.

How comfortable are you with giving him a green light on a scale of 0 to 10, where 0 is totally uncomfortable and 10 is totally comfortable?

    0   1   2   3   4   5   6   7   8   9   10

If your score is 8 or more, well done! Move to the next section – practising in real life. If your score is 7 or less, play the CD and listen to track 7 again. Keep repeating this process until you get a score of 8. Be patient, it might take five, or even ten times to get to this score.

Practising in real life

You can now start to give green lights to men that you fancy in real life. You may see these types of men quite often or you may see them quite rarely. However, your mind is now primed to be much more comfortable with giving them a green light. Next time you see a guy you fancy:

- use your peripheral vision to keep an eye on him
- catch his eye, hold eye contact and say in your head, 'You are really gorgeous'
- look away
- catch his eye, smile and hold eye contact and say in your head, 'You are really gorgeous'
- give yourself a score on a scale of 0 to 10 on how comfortable you are with doing this.

If the score is below 8, as soon as you get home put on the CD and listen to track 7, using this example for the track. Repeat the CD until you have a score of 8 or higher.

The more you practise, the better you become and the easier it will be to give green lights. The aim is to get you to the stage where you automatically give out a green light when you see a person you fancy.

Some people find giving green lights really easy. Other people find it quite a challenge and they need lots of practice. Remember that giving a green light is the key flirting skill; it is the first step in starting to flirt.

Case study

Mizuke was completely uncomfortable with giving green light signals through eye contact. This was mainly because of her cultural background, where giving direct eye contact was discouraged. In her whole life, she had never chosen a man she fancied, and then got him to approach her.

Mizuke went through all off the above steps, getting comfortable with giving green lights one stage at a time. Finally, when she was completely comfortable with giving green lights and her timing was perfect, she left my office. Thirty minutes later she called, 'Oh my god, I exchanged phone numbers with a guy, oh my god!'

Men – spotting the green light

The most important flirting skill that I can teach a man is to spot green lights. As we have seen, the basics of flirting are incredibly simple. The majority of the time, it is women who select their potential partners. As a man, it is your job to spot the women who are interested in you and then take action.

You may not realize that these green light signals are going off all around you. Most people think that women aren't really checking out men that much. They don't appreciate that everywhere they go, there are green light signals being flashed at them. What is great about learning to spot green light signals is that women don't always consciously realize that they are giving green light signals. Eye contact, for most women, is something that they don't think about. When they fancy someone, they look in their direction, catch a man's eye, look away and then look back again. Men have to learn to spot these signals, and most men are not looking for them!

Case studies

Stuart learned about green light signals and then went for a walk in Covent Garden in London. He was amazed – he received more attention in two hours than he had in the last two years. The green lights were going off all around him – he just hadn't seen them before.

Stephen was just the same. He never realized when a woman was interested. He would go into bars, parties and look around at work, and it seemed to him that he could never tell if a woman was interested or not. After one session of learning green light signals, he was amazed. Now he sees green lights everywhere, in the street, in bars, on public transport and at work.

Why do so many men seem to have signal blindness? Everyone can see a green light when they are driving. Why is it that men can't see the green light signals that women are giving all the time? The answer is pretty simple: men are never taught what the signals mean, and they are never taught to look for the green lights. Many of my clients have seen green lights but they just don't really understand what they mean. Most men will notice women catching their eye. Frequently, however, they feel that the eye contact did not last long and they didn't really know what it meant.

One thing you need to know now: women don't catch a man's eye by mistake. Or, if they do, they certainly don't do it a second time by mistake. Women, from an early age, have learned that if they catch a man's eye, certain types of men will come straight up to them and start trying to chat them up. Most women, at least unconsciously, know about the power of eye contact.

So, you must remember:

- if a woman catches your eye once, it is for a reason; she is giving you an orange light signal
- if a woman catches your eye for a second time, then it is also for a reason; she is giving you a green light signal
- a green light is an invitation to start a conversation with a woman.

According to psychologists' studies, there is probably good reason why men miss the green signals that women give. When a woman first sees a man, she looks at him from the head down. When a man first sees a woman, he looks at her from the feet upwards and then he moves on to her face.

It doesn't take too much imagination to understand what happens. While a woman is giving her orange light signal and looking at a man's face, the man is not looking at her face. This is one of the main reasons that men seem to miss the first orange light signal.

To be blunt, men spend a lot of time looking at women's bodies rather than at their faces. Instead of keeping an eye out for that crucial green light, men are checking out a woman's assets and so they also miss the green light signal.

It is vital that you:

• Look at a woman's face first – this makes it more likely that you will catch the first orange light
• Avoid staring at her body – better still, use your peripheral vision and keep an eye out for her looking your way. Then you can turn and catch her green light.

Exercise

• When you are walking down the street, look at a woman's face first. As soon as you see a woman who you think you might be attracted to, look at her face first.
• When the woman gets closer and is just about to pass you, make sure you that you look at her face again.

How long is long enough?

A common question that men have about eye contact is: how long is long enough? Often men say to me that they have noticed some eye contact, but they are not sure if it lasted long enough. The rule is very simple. If you notice a woman catching your eye, then the eye contact is long enough. Any direct eye contact is long enough – that should be your rule of thumb. The longer it lasts, the better.

Some may say that a person will hold your eye contact for three seconds or more. This is just not true. There are few people who will give such direct eye contact. Trust me. However, if a woman catches your eye, then it is for a reason.

Past green lights

A good place to start with spotting green lights is to think about the past. Think about when you were given eye contact and you didn't really know what it meant.

Exercise

Right now, think back to the last time that you noticed a woman catching your eye, even if it was very briefly.

Right now, write down the last time a woman caught your eye once.

....

....

Think back to what you thought it meant at the time. Write this down.

....

....

Now look back at the situation. Think about what I have told you about orange and green lights. Do you know now what that eye contact meant? Write it down now.

....

....

Now think about a situation when a woman caught your eye twice. Even if the eye contact didn't last long at all. Write this down, even if the eye contact was very, very brief.

....

....

Think back to what you thought it meant at the time. Write this down.

....

....

Now look back at the situation. Think about what I have told you about orange and green lights. Do you know now what that eye contact meant? Write it down.

....

....

Future green lights

Exercise

Imagine that you are at a party, a friend's party. Look around, listen to the sounds of your friends talking, and enjoy the great feeling of being there. You look across the room and notice a woman that you find attractive. Look at her face first. Use your peripheral vision to keep an eye on her. She turns towards you and very briefly makes eye contact. Keep looking at her with your peripheral vision. She turns and very briefly makes eye contact with you a second time.

Right now, write down what this means.

....

....

Really believing green lights

I can tell you that a woman catching your eye is a green light, but you really need to believe this. You need your brain to respond every single time that you see a girl giving you eye contact with the thought, 'Ah ha! She just gave me a green light'.

Exercise

Right now, think about something that you know gives a completely clear signal that you have to move forward – for instance, a green traffic light when you are driving.

Right now, write down how you know that you are getting a clear signal to move forward when you see a green traffic signal when driving.

....

....

Right now, circle how sure you are that you are getting a signal to move forward in your car on a scale of 0 to 10, where 0 is not sure at all and 10 is totally sure.

0   1   2   3   4   5   6   7   8   9   10

Imagine a woman catching your eye quickly and looking away. Then she catches your eye again. Circle how sure you are that this is a green light, on a scale of 0 to 10, where 0 is not at all sure and 10 is totally sure that it is a green light.

0   1   2   3   4   5   6   7   8   9   10

Right now, play your CD and listen to track 8 – believing in green lights.

Now you have listened to the CD, imagine a woman catching your eye quickly and looking away, and then catching your eye again. Circle how sure you are that this is a green light, on a scale of 0 to 10, where 0 is not at all sure and 10 is totally sure that it is a green light.

0   1   2   3   4   5   6   7   8   9   10

Right now, listen to track 8 again.

When you have listened to the CD again, imagine a woman catching your eye quickly, looking away and then catching your eye again. Circle how sure you are this is a green light, on a scale of 0 to 10, where 0 is not at all sure and 10 is totally sure that it is a green light.

0   1   2   3   4   5   6   7   8   9   10

Right now, listen once more to track 8.

When you have listened to the CD again, imagine a woman catching your eye quickly, looking away, and then catching your eye again. Circle how sure you are this is a green light, on a scale of 0 to 10, where 0 is not at all sure and 10 is totally sure that it is a green light.

0   1   2   3   4   5   6   7   8   9   10

Right now, listen again to track 8. When you have listened to the CD again, imagine a woman catching your eye quickly, looking away, and then catching your eye again. Circle how sure you are this is a green light, on a scale of 0 to 10, where 0 is not at all sure and 10 is totally sure that it is a green light.

0   1   2   3   4   5   6   7   8   9   10

Right now, listen to track 8 again. When you have listened to the CD once more, imagine a woman catching your eye quickly, looking away, and then catching your eye again. Circle how sure you are this is a green light, on a scale of 0 to 10, where 0 is not at all sure and 10 is totally sure that it is a green light.

0   1   2   3   4   5   6   7   8   9   10

This is your final score. Look back to your first score opposite. How does your first green light score compare with your final score?

When you think about a woman giving you a green light, how does it look, sound and feel? Write this down.

....

....

You should now notice that you are starting to believe that when a woman catches your eye she is giving you the signal to move forward.

06

next steps

In this chapter you will learn:
- how men and women can make the next move
- about opening lines for men
- about opening lines for women.

Making the move

For women

With flirting, it is still the men who actually make the move of starting a first conversation. As a woman, you have made the first move by giving the man a green light signal. It is now the man's job to take action and do something about it.

In certain cultures, the men are quite shy. They need a little help with making the move. You need to make it as easy as possible for them to be able to approach you and start a conversation. There are several ways in which you can do this.

- Break away from your group and go somewhere where he can start up a conversation with you. For instance, grab a drink at the bar; move to a section in the bookstore where it is easy for him to approach you.
- Keep giving him small amounts of eye contact. Catch his eye every now and then to make sure that he knows you are still interested.

Don't:

- hang around in a big group with your friends – this is intimidating. There is no way that he will approach you in a big group of friends.

Remember that you might need to be patient. For some men it is a scary prospect to approach a woman and start a conversation.

Make the move yourself

Some studies (e.g. the Kate Fox research study, see p. 2 for details) have shown that women who approach men directly are perceived as more sexually available. If you want to avoid this perception, and your man isn't making the move, then you can make an indirect approach. Approach him under the guise of doing something else. You can:

- ask for the time
- ask for advice
- ask for directions.

This is essentially just an excuse for you to approach him first and make it seem like there is some other reason. This then bypasses the problem of seeming too sexually available or aggressive.

For men

So, you have received the green light signal from a woman. She's caught your eye! What next? This point in the flirting process seems to be the most challenging for men. Let's call it the 'bungee' moment. It is the point where you have to commit to starting a conversation. This is the stage in flirting when most men fall by the wayside or struggle. If you are lucky enough to feel comfortable starting a conversation, get going. If not, let's talk about the bungee moment.

Bungee jumping

Starting a conversation with a woman who fancies you is a little like bungee jumping. It is normally safe, but it is something that people may find terrifying. For most people, it is no use telling them to make the move, they actually need some sort of tool to get them moving. As with bungee jumping, you are standing at the edge and you need something to help push you over. Otherwise you might just stand there in terror.

Many people stand just at the edge. They make excuses about why they aren't jumping. The point is that once you jump, then everything happens from there. It is exciting and exhilarating.

Case study

Lee's football team reached the semi-final of the FA Cup in the UK. The semi-final game was a good example of a bungee moment – there was a long history of failure and fear of failure (the team had never made it into the semi-final before). There was great tension in the crowd – it seemed impossible to them that the team could actually make it through.

Suddenly there was a breakthrough; the team scored the winning goal. Lee and the crowd went completely berserk. There was a huge sense of elation and relief for Lee, knowing that his team had succeeded. This is a great illustration of a bungee moment – there is fear and anticipation beforehand and then there is huge excitement and relief afterwards.

The bungee moment is a natural part of the flirting process. There is always going to be a little bit of fear involved, and a rush of adrenalin when you make the jump. Here is an exercise that will help you start to make that jump.

Exercise

Right now, think about a time when you did something that scared you, but you felt exhilarated once you'd done it. Something where you had a bungee moment. Maybe it was at work, doing sport, or watching sport, for example.

Right now, write down your bungee moment.

....

Right now, remember that moment vividly. Write down what you saw, felt and heard.

....

....

Right now, remember the point when you just were about to make the 'jump'. Write it down.

....

....

Right now, remember the feeling after the 'jump'. Write down exactly how it looked, felt and sounded.

....

....

Right now, think about starting a conversation with a woman that you want to flirt with. Think about the bungee moment, and write down how it looks, sounds and feels.

....

....

Right now, write down how scared you feel about the flirting bungee moment on a scale of 0 to 10, where 0 is not at all scared, and 10 is totally scared.

0   1   2   3   4   5   6   7   8   9   10

Right now, play the CD and listen to track 9 – bungee jumping.

Right now, write down how scared you feel about the flirting bungee moment on a scale of 0 to 10, where 0 is not at all scared, and 10 is totally scared.

0   1   2   3   4   5   6   7   8   9   10

Right now, listen to track 9 again.

Right now, write down how scared you feel about the flirting bungee moment on a scale of 0 to 10, where 0 is not at all scared, and 10 is totally scared.

0   1   2   3   4   5   6   7   8   9   10

Right now, listen once more to track 9.

Right now, write down how scared you feel about the flirting bungee moment on a scale of 0 to 10, where 0 is not at all scared, and 10 is totally scared.

0   1   2   3   4   5   6   7   8   9   10

Right now, listen again to track 9.

Right now, write down how scared you feel about the flirting bungee moment on a scale of 0 to 10, where 0 is not at all scared, and 10 is totally scared.

0   1   2   3   4   5   6   7   8   9   10

Right now, listen to track 9 again.

Right now, write down how scared you feel about the flirting bungee moment on a scale of 0 to 10, where 0 is not at all scared, and 10 is totally scared.

0   1   2   3   4   5   6   7   8   9   10

Right now, compare this with your first score on the previous page.

Right now, think about the idea of starting a conversation with a woman that you want to flirt with. Think about the bungee moment, and write down how it looks, sounds and feels. Notice any differences or changes and write these down.

....

....

This exercise will make it a little easier for you to act at the bungee jump moment. You should have noticed that your score for the bungee moment has gone down by 1 or perhaps even more. Keep repeating the CD (track 9) until your bungee moment is down to 2 or 3, or even 1.

Opening lines

Now that you have spotted or given the green light signal, it is time to get the conversation started.

For men

The key thing to remember with opening lines is that corny chat-up lines just don't work. The only people for which such approaches work are super-confident, and even for them it's a case of sinking or swimming.

With an opening line, make the comment as pedestrian as possible. If you are standing at a bus stop, saying 'Is heaven missing an angel?' is clearly going to make you seem like an idiot. Asking a woman if your bus has come yet and how long she has been waiting is going to be a lot easier! A good opening line should be about something else other than the person you are chatting up. You both know that you are flirting – it is a matter of taking things one step at a time.

The weather comment

The weather comment is a great opening line. You're commenting about something in your environment, and inviting a response from the other person. You can literally start a conversation with a comment about the weather. Imagine you are standing at the bus stop and it is pouring with rain. The person next to you has given you a green light. 'Awful weather!' you might say. This is a good opening line because it is impersonal. The person has a choice about whether they want to respond or not. If they aren't interested in talking to you, they won't answer, or the response will be short.

If they are interested in talking to you, they will respond with some enthusiasm: 'Isn't it grim? I hear it's going to be raining for the next couple of days!' You have just opened the door to a great flirting conversation.

You can use a weather comment with any sort of situation; weather comments are only limited by your imagination! In a hot bar, you can make a comment about that. The service is lousy; make a comment about that. It is simply about making some sort of comment about a shared experience that you are both having. You both know that you are starting a flirtatious conversation – but you are giving the woman an easy choice about whether to continue or not.

Examples of weather comments:

- 'Phew, it's hot today!'
- 'Awful weather!'
- 'It's stuffy in here.'
- 'The service is terrible here!'

Widgets

Widgets are also a great way to start a conversation. There are two types of widgets: personal widgets and impersonal widgets.

Impersonal widgets are the best ones to start with. Say you are in an art gallery. You are standing next to the person that you would like to start talking to. You might like to make a comment about the painting; this is an impersonal widget. You are in a bar and there is a great band playing. 'Great set this evening', you might say. Again, this is an impersonal widget. You are making a comment about something you can both see or hear.

Examples of impersonal widgets:

- picture at an art gallery
- beautiful sunset
- busy traffic
- large sculpture
- a DJ.

Personal widgets make it clearer that you are interested in the person you are talking to. You need to pick something that they are wearing – like their top, an interesting watch they are wearing or their necklace, and then make a comment about that: 'Great necklace'.

The danger with the personal widget is that you make it clear from the start that you are flirting with them. The woman then has to decide, then and there, whether they fancy you or not – which means they will either decide yes or no. If you use a weather comment or an impersonal widget, it is more comfortable because you are just starting a conversation that could lead anywhere. With a personal widget, it is clear that you are flirting from the start.

For women

It is also possible for women to use opening lines, but generally they should be more indirect than the ones used by men. As a woman, you can take the direct approach and use either weather comments or widgets (see previous sections), but there is a danger that a man will find that a little intimidating, or think that you are sexually available. Better to try some of the following suggestions instead.

Asking for information

This is an oldie but a goldie. You simply need to ask the person that you want to flirt with for some information. Information about directions, about where to find something in the shop where you are etc. You can also ask people the time.

The trick is that once you have the information, you have to move the conversation on to the next level. Otherwise, they will give you the information and keep walking! This is just a matter of asking another question, like 'Where are you from?' Ask for information about:

- directions
- best buys
- the time
- where to buy tickets, etc.

Asking for advice

Asking for advice is one of the easiest ways for a woman to discreetly start a conversation with a man. The beauty about asking for advice is that men love to give it. Think about the context you are in, and then ask some advice related to that context.

For instance, I once took some of my clients dog-racing. They spotted a guy that they fancied, then wandered up and asked for some advice about dog-racing. They played the innocent first-timer, and the guy was happy to give them loads of advice about how to bet, which dogs to bet on, etc. The conversation then moved on and they were happily chatting for ages.

It is a matter of adjusting your advice for your surroundings. For example, if you are away on holiday, you might like to ask some advice about the best places to visit in the local area. If you are in a shop, you could ask advice on the best stereo system to purchase. Or you might like the old ploy of 'I'm buying a present for my brother, what do you think about...?'

Ask for advice about:

- the place where you are
- top places to visit
- the best food on the menu
- the best drinks in the pub
- how something works.

In summary:

- Generally women give a green light to men then initiate conversation.
- Women should initiate conversation indirectly.
- Opening lines work best if they are mundane, use weather comments, widgets, asking for information and advice.

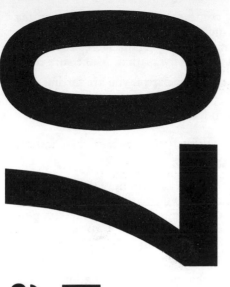

07

hit the flirting accelerator

In this chapter you will learn:
- about body language basics
- how to make it clear that you fancy someone
- about the basic signals that show someone likes you.

Once you have started the conversation, it is time to turn the flirting heat up and take things further. First, go back and run through Chapter 3 on flirting every day again. Here are the first and most crucial steps to a flirty conversation. Make sure that:

- you are completely focused on the person you are flirting with
- you listen with passion
- you make the other person feel important.

Body language basics

If you are having a flirtatious conversation, how do you take it to the next level? The easiest way to move flirting on is through body language. However, body language can be quite complex and challenging to remember. Ideally, you want to be enjoying the flirting rather than worrying about what sort of body language signals you are giving off.

It is most effective to change what you are thinking rather than what you are doing when it comes to body language. When you change what you think and feel, then your body language automatically follows. Having flirtatious thoughts is a good way to do this. Working with my clients, I have found the following to be the best techniques for getting your flirting body language going.

Stage 1 – admire what you find attractive in them

The first stage is to spend some time working out what you find attractive in the person you are flirting with. Is it their eyes? Spend time thinking about why you like their eyes. Look into their eyes, look at the details and why they make you feel attracted to that person. Is it their body? Look at their body. Go through the reasons why you find them attractive. Take your time. Really enjoy everything you find attractive about them.

By doing this your body language will start to change. You will subtly give signals that you find them attractive because of your eye contact. They won't quite know what is going on, but they will start to get the message that you are flirting with them!

Stage 2 – kiss the person you fancy in your mind

When you are talking to someone you fancy, don't focus so much on the conversation. Look at their lips. Imagine what it would be like to kiss them. Imagine this in a lot of detail. Think about exactly what it would feel like. Take your time. Run through a whole movie of kissing them, right from the initial gentle touching of lips to getting passionate. They won't know exactly what you are thinking about, but they will subconsciously get the hint that you fancy them. The signals you give off are actually quite subtle, and the person you are flirting with won't really know quite what is going on – for some reason, they will feel like they fancy you more, but they won't be able to put their finger on the reason why.

Stage 3 – undress the person in your mind

The next level really turns up the heat. Once you have imagined kissing the person in detail, start to think about what it would be like to slowly undress them. Imagine this in detail. Undo each individual button on their top. Slowly and gently help slide it off.

What you are thinking about will be subtly reflected in your body language. Again the person you are flirting with won't quite know what's going on, but subconsciously they will. For some reason, they will start to fancy you more and perhaps realize that you fancy them.

Just by thinking about kissing someone, your body language is changing. Your eyelids are probably dropping a little lower. Perhaps your cheeks are flushing and you might be feeling hot. Also if you imagine kissing them in a lot of detail, your lips and skin may be starting to feel more sensitive. It's likely that blood has also rushed to your lips and they are looking redder. These are all subtle flirtatious signals that show that we like someone – and you have managed to give them simply by thinking about kissing someone.

Five signs they like you

So we've covered the ways to start giving the signals that you fancy someone but what about the signals that they fancy you? I will go into some more detail in Chapter 8, but here it is useful to learn about some of the basic signs and signals. There are five important signs to keep an eye out for.

1. The flirting triangle

When you are having a conversation with someone, normally your eyes move back and forward between the other person's eyes in a straight line. When someone fancies you, this straight line turns into a flirting triangle. They will start to look at your lips. The more they look at your lips, the more they fancy you. If they fancy you even more, the flirting triangle will expand, often moving down to your chest, and sometimes even lower. The bigger the flirting triangle, and the more time they spend looking at your lips or below, the better!

2. You mirror one another

People like people who are similar to them. You can literally see this when two people are getting on well because they 'mirror' one other. Basically, the other person's body language will be similar to yours. One hand on your waist? They will do this too. Your feet pointed towards them? They will be doing the same. Leaning in? They will lean in. You can test to see if someone is mirroring you by deliberately changing position. If things are going well, they will follow suit and change to the same position within about a minute.

3. Feet point towards you

In body language, feet are a great indicator of the direction in which a person wants to go. People tend to be unaware of their body language below the waist, they have read about crossing or uncrossing their arms, or which way their chest is facing, but the feet almost always point to where their interest lies.

Quickly glance to see where the feet of the person you are talking to are pointing. If they are both pointing towards you, or mirroring your feet position, it's good news. If they are pointing away from you, it indicates that the person's interest is elsewhere and they would probably like to move on.

4. They raise their eyebrows

This is quite a subtle signal to catch, but it is a good indicator because it is virtually impossible to fake. When a person first sees you, if they raise their eyebrows they are showing their interest. It's a good sign.

5. Green light

Back to basics. If a person catches your eye, then looks back, you are getting a green light. When you are talking, if they are interested, they will also maintain strong eye contact.

Practise flirting with them

Now it's time to put this all into practice in the gym of your mind. You are going to imagine vividly putting into practice what you have just learned.

Exercise

Right now, write down the name of a person that you fancy and you would like to practise flirting with.

....

Right now, play the CD and listen to track 10 – practising flirting.

Practise with this track for as long as it takes you to be comfortable with visualizing this with someone you fancy.

In summary:

• The way you think changes your body language.
• Admire what you find attractive in them, kiss them and undress them in your mind.
• Keep an eye out for the flirting triangle, mirroring, where their feet point, raised eyebrows and green lights.
• Practice makes perfect.

08

signs and sins

In this chapter you will learn:
- about the different zones
- how to test how a person feels about you
- flirting signs from men and women
- deadly flirting sins.

Different zones

In this chapter, I cover the body language that will tell you when someone you are flirting with is interested in you. Working with clients, I find that it sometimes takes a while to remember all the body language signs and so I have developed a quick and easy method for testing how much someone likes you.

You need to understand that people have 'zones'. Usually people think of their 'zones' as their personal space. Zones are very powerful things. The first zone is the 'public zone' – which is at about arm's length. This is the distance where you could comfortably reach out and touch someone with your arm fully extended. We are generally comfortable keeping this distance from strangers. It is possibly the origin of the phrase 'keep them at arm's length'.

Closer than arm's length is the 'personal zone'. This is the place that we reserve for people who are friends, familiar, or who we are starting to fancy. One of the clever things that you might notice about loud bars and clubs is that to talk, you need to get very close to someone – forcing you inside their personal zone in order to be heard. You will find this type of enforced intimacy comfortable if you like the person or uncomfortable if you don't.

When you get within a hand's length of a person, about 15–30 cm, this is their 'intimate zone'. This is the place where they only let people who are very close, either friends or lovers.

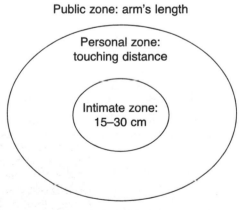

Public zone: arm's length

Personal zone: touching distance

Intimate zone: 15–30 cm

Figure 3 Zones

Zones are very powerful things and you must treat them with respect. Get too close too quickly and you will repulse someone – stay too far away and you won't seem to be showing interest. Think about being squashed on public transport. One of the main things that makes it so stressful and traumatic is that strangers are literally being forced into your personal zone. This is an uncomfortable experience for most people.

You can quickly and easily use zones to test how close a person wants you to get.

In summary:

- People have different 'zones' that they usually think of as 'personal space'.
- Arm's length or further is your 'public zone'.
- Arm's length or closer is your 'private zone'.
- One hand's length away is your 'intimate zone'.
- Zones are powerful and you must treat them with respect.

Testing how they feel about you

When flirting with someone, you should start just outside their personal zone – that is at about arm's length. If you think things are going well, test it. Lean inside their personal zone, and see how they respond. If they feel comfortable, they will either stay still or, even better, they will match what you are doing and lean closer. If they lean back, it means you are moving too fast.

Once you move closer, and if the other person is comfortable, stay there for a little while. When you feel comfortable again, try moving closer again. Watch how the other person responds. If they move back, back off – move to your previous distance.

This way, step by step, you can see how comfortable a person is with you moving closer. Once you move inside their personal zone, take it slowly. If things are going well, they might be comfortable with you going into their intimate zone.

This technique is one of the quickest, easiest and simplest ways to test the signs to see whether a person is interested in you or not.

One caveat – you must make sure that the other person has an escape route and can move away from you comfortably. If you pin them up against a bar or wall, there is nowhere for them to go if they don't feel comfortable with you getting close!

In summary:

- When flirting, start in the public zone.
- Lean inside the other person's personal zone and see how they respond.
- If they stay still or match you, it's a good sign.
- Step by step move closer as the other person feels comfortable.
- Take it slowly – move too fast and you will scare the other person off!
- Make sure the other person has an escape route.

Signs from men

It is worth keeping an eye out for key flirting signals. If a man fancies a woman, he will be giving signals that show what he's thinking. If you notice four more of these signs, you can be pretty much be sure he fancies you.

According to the international body language expert Tracey Cox, the following are sure signs that things are going well.

- *He'll become an attention seeker* – when a guy fancies you, he will try and attract your attention. This might mean he suddenly seems to become louder and more boisterous or he makes exaggerated movements and gestures. He might also stand slightly apart from his friends.
- *He'll play with his hair* – if a guy fancies you, he will involuntarily 'preen' trying to make himself look good for you.
- *He'll show off his body* – when a guy fancies you he will stand taller and perhaps slightly puff out his chest.
- *He'll show off the crown jewels* – men don't realize this, but when they are around women they fancy, they unconsciously spread their legs, showing you what's on offer.
- *He'll start undressing* – when we fancy someone, we unconsciously start undressing. If he starts undoing buttons, or taking off his jacket, then he is starting something he would probably like to finish in your bedroom.
- *His hands will go on his hips* – unconsciously he is making himself look bigger, which suggests confidence. Also, humans point towards what they want people to see, so you might notice his fingers pointing towards his groin.
- *He'll start touching himself* – when we are attracted to someone, our skin, particularly our mouth, becomes more

sensitive to being touched. You might notice him touching his chin, lips or cheek more or drinking or smoking faster.

- *He'll lend you something* – this is a protective and sexy ownership gesture – he is offering something of his to you. This also means he has to hang around to get it back before the end of the night.

If you see four or more of these signs, you are on to a winner.

Signs from women

So, you've started the conversation and you need to know how well things are going. The beauty about flirting is that if you learn to look out for the right signals, then you never need to ask. Whether she fancies you is shown by her body language.

If you are chatting with a woman, there are giveaway signs if she fancies you. Again, according to Tracey Cox, see four or more of these signs and you can be almost certain that you are on to a winner.

- *She's looking at your mouth* – the more she likes you, the more time she will spend looking at your mouth. Unconsciously she's thinking about what it would be like to kiss you.
- *She's stroking herself* – when we stroke ourselves we are doing two things – drawing attention to the part being stroked, and doing to ourselves what we wish the other person was doing to us.
- *She starts touching her lips* – when we fancy someone, blood starts rushing to our lips. They become more sensitive and feel good to touch.
- *She licks her lips, fluffs her hair and generally preens* – she's telling you that she's making herself more attractive for you.
- *She whispers and leans* – by whispering, she is making you lean close and inviting you inside her personal space. We only do this with people we like.
- *She'll start putting objects in your space* – people are intensely territorial. If she likes you, rather than touching, she'll start putting her stuff closer to you. Most commonly, you'll notice her glass moving closer.
- *She flashes her wrists* – wrists are an erogenous zone. If she's interested, she'll show her yours, especially if she's smoking.

- *She starts getting undressed* – when people fancy each other, they unconsciously start to take their clothes off. She'll start taking off layers or moving her hemline up. All a hint of what she might like to be doing later on.
- *She starts stroking things* – if we fancy someone, unconsciously we generally start stroking or caressing objects. Usually it's a glass or a straw.

Deadly sins

Almost everyone has at least one or more of these deadly body language sins. Get rid of them!

- *Melting into the pavement* – stand up straight! This makes an enormous difference to how you feel and how you are perceived.
- *Looking at the floor* – look up! This makes you accessible and more open to people.
- *Leaning away from someone you like* – this tells them that you don't like them!
- *Letting it all hang out* – a little relaxed is fine, but letting it all hang out is positively unattractive!
- *Turning away from someone you fancy* – You are saying 'I am not interested' with your entire body.
- *Fiddling with your collar or scratching your neck* – this is like wearing a big sign saying 'I am nervous and uncomfortable!'
- *Propping your face up with your hand* – this tells the other person that you are bored with them, and bored with what they are saying.

In summary:

- Pay attention to people's flirting zones.
- Look out for key flirting signs.
- Avoid the flirting sins.

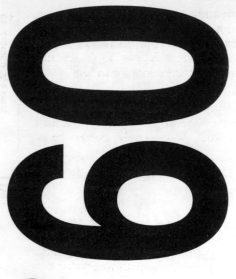

09

closing the deal

In this chapter you will learn:
- whose job it is to close the deal
- the three-step process to closing
- following up.

Once you've started the conversation, seen the signs that the are other person is interested, and had a fun conversation, it's time to close the deal. This is the most crucial part of flirting if you want to take things to the next level – if you don't get any contact details, how are you going to take it any further?

As with other parts of flirting, a lot of confusion surrounds closing the deal. Men aren't quite sure what they should do; women aren't quite sure what they should do either. As a result, the deal is often left open and never really comes to a satisfactory conclusion.

Whose job is it?

The biggest cause for not closing the deal is that there is confusion about whose job it is. Should a man just offer his phone number? Will the woman call? In this liberated day and age, men often think it is now up to the woman to ask for the phone number.

Like the rest of flirting, the best strategy is to stick to tradition. Though there may have been some changes – I have met women at singles events who are willing to ask for a phone number if they are really interested – this is the exception to the rule. Men, if you wait for a woman to ask for your phone number, you will be waiting a long time.

Whose job is it? This is simple. It's the woman's job to give the hint that she is interested, and it is the man's job to get the contact details.

Over and over again, I see these basic rules being ignored at singles nights. 'I gave her my phone number', guys tell me. 'I'll wait to see if she emails me afterwards', 'If she was interested she would have given me her phone number'. The conversations go on and on. The simple fact is that when I talk to these guys again, the women have never been in contact. They haven't called, they haven't emailed and, when I go and ask them, often they were interested but they were waiting for the guy to ask for their phone number. If you are a man, it is clearly still your job to get hold of the contact details.

If you are a woman, you can certainly take the front foot and exchange details. But make sure that you do that – offer to exchange details. A woman needs to make it blindingly obvious that she is interested in meeting up again – so obvious that it is really easy for a man to ask for her contact details.

If you are a woman, think of the man you are flirting with as a donkey. You need to dangle a big juicy carrot right in front of his nose and then let him take a bite.

If you are a man, you need to keep a sharp eye out for this carrot and, when it's there, get chomping!

In summary:
- It's a man's job to close the deal.
- As a man, you need to exchange details. You *must* get her phone number or email address. Offer her your phone number and then get hers.
- As a woman, it's your job to make it clear you are interested in taking the next step.
- As a woman, dangle the carrot right in front of him until he takes a bite!

Step by step closing

For both sides, to avoid possible embarrassment and to make sure that the carrot is being dangled in front of you, the best way to close is step by step:

- Replay the fun time you've had
- Suggest something fun
- Exchange details – it's the man's job to ask.

Replay the best bits

The first step is to have a little instant replay of the fun time that you have had. Refer back to any particularly funny or entertaining parts of the night or of your conversation. This allows you to check to see if the person is really that interested – it's a good sign if they look like they are still enjoying themselves and if they laugh again.

Are they looking bored and uninterested? Then there is not much point moving on to the next stage. The beauty is that by making closing a three-step process, you can bail out early if necessary, without the embarrassment of being turned down.

Whether you are a man or a woman, you can both replay the best bits. Women, if you are really interested in the guy, this is the equivalent of telling him that you have really enjoyed yourself and his company.

Replaying the best bits of the night also brings back the good feelings the other person has about you. When you think about something fun, or you laugh, it actually releases chemicals into your brain to make you feel good. Someone who is feeling good about you is much more likely to hand over their contact details.

Suggest something fun

During the conversation you will have picked up what the other person loves and what you have in common. You should now have some idea about what would be fun to do together next.

They love museums; suggest checking out what exhibitions are on. They are into food; suggest going out for lunch to try something new. They are into movies; suggest going to the cinema. They are an adrenalin junkie; suggest doing something exciting. Or, if you are just having a great conversation, use the golden oldie of getting together for a drink or a coffee.

By making a specific suggestion of something fun, you are making it clear that you want to take it to the next level. At the same time, you are keeping it nice and vague – you don't have to sort out times or anything right there and then.

This is the equivalent of getting out the carrot and doing the dangling. Guys, if the carrot is being dangled, then it's time to bite. Ladies, if a guy is suggesting this, then you need to make it clear that you are interested in taking things to the next level.

Don't like the suggestion, but still like the person? Maybe they made a bad choice – suggest something else. A bit of roller-blading? Going to your local park? Get out a different carrot and dangle it in front of their nose.

If the other person says yes, they are actually saying yes to handing over their contact details. After all, how can you meet up unless you have exchanged contact details? It makes the exchanging of details natural and easy. No chance of rejection, because they have already agreed to give you their contact details!

If the other person doesn't seem interested in meeting up, then they are making it clear – they don't want to hand over their contact details. This saves you the embarrassment of asking for their details and getting turned down.

Exchange details

Now it is a simple matter of exchanging details. The beauty is that they have already said yes to giving you their phone number. Otherwise, how are you going to arrange that picnic in the park or the walk by the river?

I have to make one thing crystal clear. *As a man, it is your job to ask for her phone number.* You know she is going to give it to you, so get on with it!

Exchanging details evens up the field. It suggests that either person can get in touch. And either person can but, if in doubt and if you are a man, remember you have to take the lead.

The follow-up

As a general rule, with the follow-up it is the guy who has to do the chasing. You both know where you stand, so it should be pretty clear.

Still in a little doubt? If you are a woman, you need to keep dangling that carrot. Send him a text message saying that you really enjoyed talking and look forward to hearing from him about what you discussed doing. That way you are not actually doing the chasing, but you are still keeping the carrot clearly in view. Or perhaps send him an email saying the same thing. As a woman, you need to keep the carrot dangling until he bites!

As a man, she has said yes to getting together again, so it is your job to arrange the date.

In summary:

- Replay the best bits to bring back the good feelings the other person has about you.
- Suggest something fun and see how the other person responds.
- Exchange details – make sure that you get the other person's phone number.
- As a general rule, it is the guy who has to do the chasing.

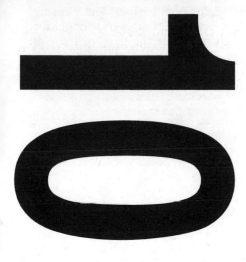

10

flirting at work

In this chapter you will learn:
- about the 'flirting zones' at work
- how to draw the line in business with non-sexual flirting
- the benefits and dangers of flirting at work.

Work can be a place for flirting, for both business and pleasure. According to a UK survey[1] of over 5,000 workers, people flirt more at work than in supermarkets, at the gym or even on holiday. Women and men are almost equally flirtatious at work – 72 per cent of men have flirted at work compared to 69 per cent of women. Twenty-eight per cent of men and women have taken the flirting further.

Interestingly, people see flirting in business as a way of getting what they want done. According to the same poll, 88 per cent believed that flirting at work could help them get what they wanted done.

Flirting zones at work

According to Kate Fox, from the Social Issues Research Centre in Oxford, there are no universal rules for flirting at work as each workplace has its own set of rules.

If you are going to flirt at work, the first things you need to look for are the 'flirting zones'. These are areas and times in the office where flirting 'with intent' is seen as acceptable. The most common flirting zone is in the kitchen or around the coffee machine. Sometimes there is even a flirting zone around the photocopier.

You must realize that, at work, flirting is acceptable on certain occasions and in certain places. For example office Christmas parties are generally a flirting free for all! Another instance is morning sales meetings which may be fun and flirtatious.

Each workplace is different, so take your time to observe where the flirting zones are. Keep an eye on someone that you respect in the office who is at the same hierarchical level as you – perhaps the most respected member of your team (different management levels flirt in different places). Watch their behaviour and this will tell you where the 'flirting zones' are in the office. These are the places in which you can engage in 'flirting with intent' with colleagues that you actually fancy.

Make sure that you ignore what the 'office clown' does. It is their job to break the rules of the office for the entertainment of other people. Trying to work out flirting zones from what they do is a waste of time.

[1] A study conducted by Concepts and Ideas on behalf of the online flirting community SmartFlirts, reported in Contractor UK, 2 November 2005

Paying attention to flirting zones

Once you have established where the flirting zones are in your workplace, stick to them. They are equivalent to personal space zones (see Chapter 8). If you flirt outside of these zones, your flirting will be frowned upon and perhaps seem unprofessional.

Generally, you should only flirt with colleagues who approximately have the same status as you, or are outside your management hierarchy. Don't flirt up and don't flirt down. A USA study and online poll found that when people flirted with their superiors or with their staff, this was mostly likely to end in trouble.[2]

In business, draw the line

There is a variety of anecdotal evidence that flirting can be very good for your professional career. Flirt experts who focus on flirting at work claim that once people learn to flirt there can be dramatic changes in their performance and productivity. The key to remember is that this type of flirting is about listening and paying attention.

In the business environment, it is very important to be able to draw the line between sexual flirting and non-sexual flirting. You will see in the next section that if you use sexual flirting in business, it can actually be detrimental to your career in the long term. The essence of non-sexual flirting is to use the techniques you have worked through earlier.

1 Listen with complete attention. Pretend that the person you are speaking with is the most important person in the world.
2 Make the other person feel important. Imagine that there is a huge flashing light above their head saying, 'Make me feel important'.

You might like to go back and repeat the exercises in the 'Listening' and 'Making people feel important' sections in Chapter 3.

With non-sexual flirting, you have to learn to draw the line. This is drawing a verbal line in the sand with the person you are flirting with, making it clear that you are not sexually available. Do you ever wonder why women seem to be able to flirt with gay men so easily? Well, a clear sexual line has been drawn in

[2]Best Life Magazine, online poll of 1,451 women, 15 February 2006, reported on www.careerbuilder.com
Flirting in the Workplace, 1 March 2005, *Gender and Society*, Sage Publications, Inc.

the sand – there is no way that sex can be involved, so everyone just relaxes and has fun.

In your business flirting, if you suspect that someone thinks you are flirting with them because you fancy them, draw a line. There is a variety of ways to do this. The easiest is to make it clear that you are already spoken for:

• Mention your boyfriend/girlfriend.
• Mention your husband/wife.

This makes it clear that you are taken, and it makes it much easier to sit back, relax and flirt. Even if you don't have a boyfriend or girlfriend, you can make one up.

The dangers of sexual flirting at work

While flirting at work can help to build relationships and further your career, you must be very careful to avoid sexual flirting to get what you want. The danger is that if you use sexual flirting to get what you want, you will be perceived as less competent. This is backed up by research. A study by Tulane University of female MBA (Master of Business Administration) graduates, aged 25 to 60, found that sexual flirting actually had a measurably detrimental effect on their careers.[1] Forty-nine per cent of the women admitted that they used sexual conduct to try and get what they wanted, which included crossing their legs provocatively, wearing short skirts and massaging men's shoulders. The women who used this type of sexual flirting were promoted, on average, 33 per cent less, and were also paid 25 per cent less than those women who 'never' engaged in this sort of sexual flirting.

In summary:

• Sexual flirting can make you seem less professional and can be detrimental to your career.
• Draw the line and stick to non-sexual flirting in business.
• Pay attention to the office flirting zones.

[1]Reported on www.cnn.com, 8th August 2005.

11

speed-date flirting

Flirting when speed-dating is a specialist art. It is different from normal flirting as you have such a short time to make a first impression: three minutes. Actually, you have even less time to make a first impression as most women make up their minds about a potential partner when speed-dating in 30 seconds or less.

What not to do!

The biggest mistake you can make when you are speed-dating is to treat it like a job interview. There are a surprising number of speed-daters out there who do exactly this, particularly women. It is easy to fall into the job interview trap. After all, 20–30 speed-dates in one night can be pretty exhausting, and you can lapse into asking boring, standard questions.

The biggest turn-off in speed-dating is to ask the standard question: 'What do you do?' Work is a boring topic, unless you have an incredibly interesting job, and even then it is risky territory. You may have great chemistry, but the other person's job may be an instant turn-off. You only have three minutes, so use them wisely and leave work out of it. When speed-dating, talking about work is banned!

It's all about chemistry – keep it casual

Speed-dating is all about chemistry. It is about sitting down with a person, having a light fun chat and seeing if there is any connection between the two of you. It is not a job interview, nor a stage play. It is about having a chat with someone and making a quick decision about whether you want to see them again.

When you meet someone for the first time, you will get an instant first impression. You know if there is chemistry or not. Usually, if there is chemistry, you end up chatting to the person for much longer and then taking it from there. Speed-dating is an accelerated version of this process.

You won't learn about chemistry if you have a boring chat about their job. You will find out if there is chemistry through a casual conversation – start by asking some fun and interesting questions.

Learn from the world's first speed-dating experiment

It is useful to have a look at the results of the world's first large-scale, speed-dating experiment. It was run by Professor Richard Wiseman at the Edinburgh Science Festival in the UK.

The results from the experiment showed that women make up their minds about their dates much more quickly than men and also showed some of the best chat-up lines.

The experiment involved 100 members of the public taking part in 500 speed-dates. Each participant rated the attractiveness of the people they dated, and also indicated if they would like to meet up again.

Forty-five per cent of women reached final decisions about their potential mates in less than 30 seconds. In comparison, only 22 per cent of men made up their minds in the same time. Professor Wiseman commented that in speed-dating, men only have a few seconds to impress women – which makes their opening comments particularly important. Women were also twice as picky as men, the men ticked twice as many 'yes' boxes as the women. The top male and female speed-daters had a 100 per cent success rate – with all of their dates wanting to meet up again.

The effectiveness of opening comments was analysed by looking at the highly successful and most unsuccessful speed-daters. The most successful got their dates to talk about themselves in an unusual or quirky way. The top rated female asked, 'What's your favourite pizza topping?' The top rated man asked, 'If you were appearing on *Stars in your Eyes* [a UK talent programme], who would you be?' Those who failed made statements like, 'I have a PhD in computing' or used clichés such as 'Do you come here often?'

The best topics for conversation were also analysed – travel came out trumps, and movies came out bottom. Apparently, since men and women have such different taste in movies, this topic increased their chances of disagreement. Conversations about travel and dream destinations made people feel good and appear more attractive.

You should have a fun and interesting opening line to get the person you are speed-dating to open up and talk about themselves. Other examples you could try are as follows:

For men to women:

- 'If you were a character in the TV show *Sex and the City*, which one would you be and why?'
- 'If you were a movie star, who would you be and why?'

For women to men:

- 'If you were a superhero, which one would you be and why?'
- 'What's your favourite beer?'
- 'What's your favourite sports team?'

All these are light-hearted and will mark you out from the rest of the crowd.

Talk about something interesting

Try to get the person you are speed-dating to talk about something interesting, something that they love. In the speed-dating study, travel came out top because it made people seem glamorous and they felt good talking about it.

Another good way of getting people to open up is to find out what their passion is. It is different for everyone: some people love books, some are *Star Wars* fans, some love food, some love travel. If you can quickly find out what someone's passion is, then your three minutes will be packed full of conversation and they will be reluctant to leave.

How do you do this? Try asking, 'What's your passion?' or 'What do you do for kicks?' When people talk about something they love, it is terribly interesting for them since we all love talking about out passions, and it will make them feel good. If you have that passion in common, it means you are going to make a very quick and strong connection.

It's about your state of mind

Speed-dating is also about your state of mind. 93 per cent of communication is non-verbal – what you are feeling and thinking is reflected in your body language and voice tone. In speed-dating, you only have a short time to make a first impression, and so it is important that you are feeling confident and relaxed. When you are confident and relaxed you will find that you talk more slowly – but remember less is more – while there may be fewer words, there is more information coming from your body.

Case study

Patrick was having no luck with speed-dating. He was nervous about it and lacked confidence. Generally, he would get two ticks out of 20 at speed-dating events. I worked with him and he learned how to change his state of mind by using a mind programming CD to feel more confident about speed-dating. As a result, his whole body language changed and he gave a much better first impression. He now gets 11–12 ticks out of 20 on a regular basis.

If you feel you need a boost in confidence for speed-dating, go to Chapter 4 and the 'shrinking violet syndrome' section and do the exercise for boosting confidence. Use speed-dating as your flirting situation.

In summary:

• Talking about work is banned – it's boring.
• It's all about chemistry – keep the conversation light and fun.
• You only have 30 seconds to make your impression.
• Ask an interesting first question.
• Find out what the other person loves and get them to talk about it.
• It's about your state of mind – being relaxed and confident makes a big difference.

12

flirting online

In this chapter you will learn:
- about giving online green lights and setting realistic expectations
- that online flirting can move very fast and sometimes very slowly
- about common mistakes and online safety.

Flirting online is another arena, like speed-dating, where the rules of flirting are slightly different because of the circumstances. One thing that you need to remember about flirting online is that the 'natural' rules of flirting are magnified on the internet. The internet is like an amplifier that makes the basic traditional flirting rituals even more powerful. That said, certain other flirting rules are completely broken online. The internet is a new social space where new social rules are developing. There is 'netiquette', but this can change in different parts of the internet. As a starting point, it is best to stick to the traditional rules of flirting; you can test and modify your flirting from there.

Case study

For the UK TV show *The Wright Stuff*, I worked with a man and a woman on their internet profiles. We wrote one good profile for both, and one bad profile for both, to test the difference.

For the man, over a period of two days, the good profile didn't receive any emails. The man's bad profile received three emails.

For the woman over a period of two days, her bad profile received 74 emails. Her good profile received over 250 emails!

The above case study is a perfect illustration of internet magnification. You will remember from the earlier chapters that it is traditionally the man's role to hunt and the woman's role to choose. On internet dating sites, you will find that this traditional flirting behaviour is magnified out of all proportion. If you are a man, you will receive no attention unless you go out and do all the chasing and hunting.

If you are an attractive women, you will be literally bombarded with propositions from men. Unfortunately, this then changes the normal flirting dynamic of the women choosing the men they like and then the men making the move. Women on the internet can be so overwhelmed by attention that they never get the chance to actually do the initial choosing!

If you make basic mistakes in your approach as a man (for example failing to do the hunting) or a woman (for instance failing to give online green lights), you may receive absolutely no attention or success!

Online green light signals

If you are a man, how can you tell that you have a green light signal from a woman? Or, if you are a woman, how can you give a green light signal to a man? Normally, you will find that you can have a list of 'favourites' on most internet dating sites – these are people whose profiles you like and who you are thinking of getting in touch with. Alternatively, you may be able to send a 'wink', which is a way to indicate interest without sending a complete email. On many internet dating websites, you can also see a list of the people who have viewed your profile.

So, if you are a man, check who has put you on their favourites list. Also check who has viewed your profile and, importantly, how many times. If they have returned more than once, that is definitely a green light. If you are on their favourites list, consider this a green light and get in touch; they have already made an initial screening and you are of interest to them so, just like getting a green light signal, it is time to make the move.

If you are a woman, make sure that you put the men that you fancy in your favourites list. Then, if you like them, and the website tracks how many visits you make to people's profiles, make sure you look at their profile more than once. You need to remember that, like in real life, men sometimes won't receive these internet green lights. Often, they don't bother to look at who has put them on their favourites list, or they don't look at who has viewed them more than once. This is the internet equivalent of signal blindness. Because of this, if possible, it is best to send someone you fancy a 'wink' – the flirting equivalent of a green light. If you can't send a 'wink', send a short email, to say hello and that you like their profile. You can leave it up to them to do the chasing from there.

As with flirting in the real world, if you are a woman, you should actively choose the men that you fancy. The temptation with online dating is to sit back and let the men contact you. Remember that you still need to do the choosing and give green lights – that way you are much more likely to find a compatible partner.

Men – it's your job to hunt

As a man, with internet magnification it is even more important that you do the hunting. Look out for the green light signals described above, but you also need to be proactive about approaching women who you fancy. With internet magnification, some women won't have time to give green light signsls, so you have to hunt for them. Simply pick out their profile and send them a short email:

- Keep it short.
- Make it thoughtful and refer to their profile.
- Refer to any common ground you have.

On the internet, dating is a numbers game. You need to email 15–20 women per week. Expect a 10–20 per cent response rate. This is normal, but if it bugs you, use track 2 – zapping rejection – on the CD.

Setting your expectations: thorns and roses

With online flirting, to find the roses you will probably go through a lot of thorns along the way. You will be surprised at the number of knock-backs and disappointments you get. This is partly created by the diversity of choicc online. If you are on an online dating website with hundreds of thousands of people to flirt with, then it makes it much easier to move on. This can be a blessing and also a curse.

If you meet someone in a bar, or at a party rather than online, you are likely to spend more time flirting with them. This is partly because there is limited choice; you will probably look around the room, and realize that they are actually a pretty good prospect. You might choose to move on, but chances are you will continue to flirt because you're not missing out on anything else.

Online, if things don't go well straight away, it is easy to do another search and find someone else to flirt with. This means that people tend to invest less time in the flirting process, and are much more fussy. Rather than having fun, if someone doesn't meet their criteria, or things aren't quite going to plan, people are more likely to move on quickly.

What does this mean for you? Well, get ready – you will receive many rejections online. Many people aren't prepared for this. They stick their hand in the rosebush and are shocked when they suddenly get pricked by all the thorns. Rather than still looking for the roses, they tend to pull their hand out and give up.

You need to go into online dating with a gardening glove on. You will come across thorns on the way, and you will get rejections. In some ways this is much easier than in real life because it is not face to face. Yet the sheer number of rejections can make it difficult to accept. You might find hundreds of thorns before you get to your rose.

Be prepared. Whenever you get a rejection online, use track 2 – zapping rejection – on the CD. Using the rejection zapper regularly will keep your rejection levels low and make looking for the rose much easier. Otherwise, the danger is that the rejections will build up and you will decide to stop flirting online. That would be a great shame, because there are roses out there; you just need protection against all the thorns.

Things can move slowly

When you are you flirting on dating websites, things can move slowly. You may find that people take three or four days or sometimes even longer to reply to emails. Frequently, it takes weeks of flirting on a website to actually set up a first date! In many ways, flirting is much easier face to face – you just decide whether you like each other and then exchange details!

Things can move fast

There are times with online flirting when things can move very fast indeed. This is particularly true if you use an instant messaging system or chat room where flirting and conversation runs at a fast pace.

Online flirting seems so anonymous that it can remove many people's inhibitions. Because of the anonymity, you will find that people reveal personal details far more quickly than they ever would face to face. All the information that you see on a person's profile would normally take quite a few dates to elicit – but you get it upfront because you are online.

When you are chatting with people online, will find that they reveal personal details quickly. If you are flirting, things can get very intense very quickly. People will say things online that they would never, ever say face to face. There are advantages and disadvantages to this. You might find moving too fast very off-putting, and moving fast can create a false sense of intimacy.

You may have shared secrets online that you have never told anyone, but when you meet face to face it can be terribly disappointing. However, it can be good to work out whether you like someone quickly, and the internet makes this possible.

Be prepared for this. When you first meet someone online, be cautious about revealing too much too soon. Move at a pace that you are comfortable with. Otherwise, you may end up regretting it.

Common mistakes

The most common mistake you can make when online flirting is to treat the internet like a completely new place where you can do anything you want and where there are no rules. Just like flirting in real life, there are also rules online. The best strategy is to stick to traditional flirting rules and use them online. Below are several case studies to illustrate some common online mistakes.

Case study

Alkesh had set up a profile on an internet dating website. He had been on the website for almost a year and had almost no results. Only a few women had emailed him, and he hadn't been out on any dates. From the emails he sent out to women (which were only a few), he received no responses.

Alkesh had a 'friendly' profile, with a 'friendly' photo, of him looking friendly and smiling. Alkesh was suffering from an online case of 'frienditis'.

I worked with him to cure his online frienditis. First, we changed his profile. Rather than a smiling close-up photo, we used several more 'manly' photos: Alkesh standing in a field, with more masculine body language resting his hands on his hips; and a shot where he looked attractive but was not smiling. We also removed all references to friendship from his profile.

Second, we changed Alkesh's tactics. It is the man's role to hunt. To start with, Alkesh was doing no hunting at all. He was waiting for the women to come to him. We worked on changing this – Alkesh picked 15 women per week to email. He sent them a short but carefully thought out email. He looked at their profile, chose some key areas where they had common interests, commented on those, and asked them an open question.

The results were dramatic. From a zero response rate to his emails, Alkesh started receiving a 45 per cent response rate. Within a week, he had arranged his first ever internet date. After the changes to his profile and his photo, he received six unsolicited emails from women. After two weeks, Alkesh made his online dating profile inactive because he wanted to concentrate on all the dates and women he had already lined up.

Case study

Mandy is a successful businesswoman from Australia. With her online flirting style, she was very upfront. She would choose a man that she liked and then send him a long, quite direct email.

Mandy's results were terrible. She received almost no responses and, from the few responses she did get, the men seemed to lose interest very quickly. Mandy was suffering from 'successitis' and she was also breaking traditional flirting rules by taking on the role of the hunter rather than giving men green light signals and letting them approach her. In addition, in her profile, Mandy mentioned that some men found her quite intimidating.

I made some simple changes to her tactics and approach, working with her. Rather than directly approaching men, she would 'favourite' them and visit their profile several times. Then she would 'wink' at them. We removed the negative references in her profile about her being intimidating.

Mandy's results improved dramatically. For every ten winks she sent, she received two to three replies. Soon she went out on her first date through the internet dating site.

The main issue with both of the above case studies is that both Alkesh and Mandy broke the basic rules of flirting and paid the price. Stick to the basic rules of flirting when you are online – remember that these rules tend to be magnified, which makes them even more important.

Safe online flirting

As with flirting in real life, it is important to take basic safety precautions when you are flirting online. The key is to be able to have the fun without the danger.

To start, you need an online flirting email address. You can get a free email account from companies such as Yahoo or Hotmail. This means that you can send all of your online flirting emails from one address, keeping them separate from your work and any personal email addresses. If, unusually, you do get someone who is abusive or strange, and they are persistent, you can simply stop your online flirting email address and start again.

Then you may want to buy an online flirting mobile phone – this can be the same as your normal flirting mobile. It is relatively cheap to buy a pay-as-you-go mobile phone. A flirting mobile phone means that you can give out a phone number, and also talk to a person you have met online without worrying about them having your home or personal mobile telephone numbers.

Never give out your personal details such as home phone, mobile number, address or, particularly, financial information. The internet is a wonderful place to flirt, but you can never really be sure who you are flirting with! Therefore, if you meet someone from online flirting, make sure that you meet in a public place. During the day is best – always start with a short date, preferably just a coffee, so that you have an excuse to leave early if things don't go so well. Tell a friend what you are doing and if in doubt, ask them to call you during the date – this gives you the perfect excuse to escape from the date if things are going badly.

Online flirting is about having the fun without the danger – take basic precautions and you will be fine.

In summary:

- The internet magnifies, and sometimes warps, traditional flirting rules.
- Give green light signals by putting the person you fancy in your favourites, visiting their profile multiple times or sending them a 'wink'.
- If you are a woman, you may need to be more direct and send a quick email saying hello.
- To find the rose you will be pricked by thorns along the way.
- Be prepared – whenever you get a rejection, use the rejection zapper.
- Be careful about revealing too much too soon online.
- When flirting online, start with the traditional rules of flirting.
- Make sure you take basic safety precautions.

13

flirting if you are gay

In this chapter you will learn:
- how to flirt if you are gay
- how to navigate the maze of bi-sexual flirting
- what flirting role you should take in what situation.

Flirting if you are gay can be quite confusing at first. Sometimes, it isn't quite clear who does what. Actually, the rules are quite clear – in both gay and lesbian flirting, one person takes on the equivalent traditional role of the man, and one takes on the equivalent traditional role of the woman. There are shades and variations within this approach but, for simplicity's sake, it is best to try and be clear about which role you are taking. Once you understand this and decide which role you are going to take, flirting becomes very easy.

If you are bi-sexual, matters are slightly more complex. You will need to adjust your flirting style depending on which sex you are flirting with, and also depending on which role you like to take. If you are clear on this, the rules are quite simple.

In all cases, you take one of two basic roles – the hunter, where you are taking the traditional male role; or the chooser, where you take on the traditional female role.

Flirting if you are a gay man

The easiest way to understand your role is to look at Figure 4 below:

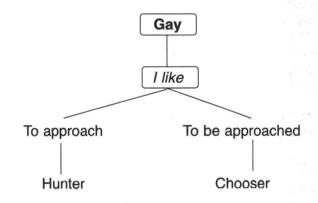

Figure 4 gay roles

Ask yourself the simple question: 'Do I like to approach other men? or do I like to choose and be approached?'

If you like to approach men, then you are taking on the hunter role. Read through the male sections of this book, and treat any man you are flirting with as having the equivalent role of a straight woman. For example, look for eye contact from a man that you fancy to spot the green light signals so that you can approach him.

If you like to choose and be approached, you are taking the chooser role. You need to give eye contact to the man that you find attractive, and make it easy for him to approach you.

Once you learn the signals, it is incredibly easy. Gay men move fast: give them a green light signal and, if they fancy you, there will be little hesitation – they will flirt with you straight away. If you are taking the hunter role, if you get a green light signal you can be assured that you will get a warm reception when you start flirting with the person who has chosen you.

Case study

Nick was frustrated that he didn't seem to be able to be successful when it came to meeting men. I worked with him on the basic signals, and he realized that he would like to choose and be approached. He learned how to give green light signals by giving the right length of eye contact to someone he fancied. We then went to a gay bar and within ten minutes he had pulled a guy he wanted.

Flirting if you are a lesbian

Look at Figure 5 below.

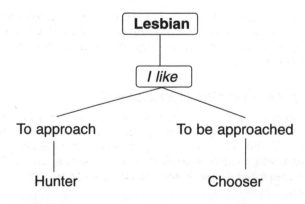

Figure 5 lesbian roles

Ask yourself the simple question: 'Do I like to approach or do I like to choose and be approached?'

If you like to approach, you are taking on the hunter role. If you like to choose and be approached, you are taking on the chooser role. There are often shades of how strongly each woman takes on this role, but flirting is easier if you are clear about which role you are taking.

Mary Hall, a San Francisco area psychologist, has been an observer and participant in lesbian courtship. She has observed that, in the past, gay women adhered to rigid gender-role models – the so-called 'butch/femme' distinction. During the 1960s, these gender roles dissolved, but in the 1990s they returned. Mary Hall now says that the roles are slightly softer and more scrambled with 'dominant femmes' and 'soft butches'. Although there are variations, women essentially either take on the equivalent of traditional female or male flirting roles (reported in Psychology Today, *The new flirting game*, Jan/Feb 1999).

Lesbian flirting can be slightly more complex than flirting between gay males as women generally tend to give signals all the time that men would interpret as flirting, for instance, they are much more tactile with each other and give more eye contact to one other. As a consequence, it can be difficult to make it clear that you are flirting with someone. The easiest tactic is to use sexual flirting signals and turn your flirting volume up to see how the other person responds.

Flirting if you are bi-sexual

Flirting if you are bi-sexual can be more complicated because you may need to change your flirting style based on the sex you are flirting with, and depending on which role you are comfortable taking.

Bi-women – hunter or chooser?

As a woman, use Figure 6 to find out if you are a hunter or chooser. For example, if you are a woman, and you fancy women, and you like to approach, then you are a hunter. If you fancy men, you are a chooser. If you fancy both, and would like to learn about flirting with women and like to be approached, you are a chooser.

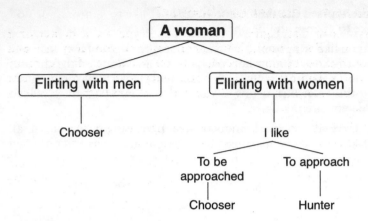

Figure 6 woman, hunter or chooser

- Chooser – take the equivalent straight female role.
- Hunter – take the equivalent straight male role.

You need to take the flirting rules outlined in this book and adapt them to your situation. To illustrate, if you are flirting with a man, you need to give him green light signals and encourage him to approach you. If you are flirting with women, and you like to approach, you need to keep an eye out for green light signals and do the approaching.

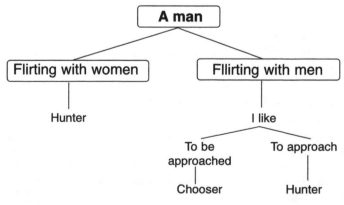

Figure 7 man, hunter or chooser

Bi-men – hunter or chooser?

As a man, use Figure 7 to find out if you are a hunter or a chooser. For example, if you are a man, and you fancy men and you like to be approached, you are a chooser. If you fancy women, you are a hunter. If you fancy both, but want to test your flirting with men and you like to be approached, you are a hunter.

- Chooser – take the equivalent straight female role.
- Hunter – take the equivalent straight male role.

Adapt your flirting style to the situation you are in. If you are flirting with women, look for green light signals and make the approach. If you are flirting with a man and you like to be approached, give him a green light signal and encourage him to approach you. The same goes for all the other material in this book. Simply adapt the appropriate material based on what role you are taking.

In summary:

- If you are a gay man or a lesbian, you will either take the 'hunter' or 'chooser' role in flirting.
- If you are bi-sexual, you will need to adapt your flirting style based on the sex of the person that you are flirting with and depending on the role you like to take.

14

flirting for students

In this chapter you will learn:
- about flirting as a student
- what specific techniques and areas you need to focus on
- how to make friends at university using flirting.

The traditional flirting tactics for most students are pretty much as follows:

- Go out with your mates to the university bar or a party.
- Get incredibly drunk.
- End up going home with anyone who is drunk enough to go home with you.
- If you are really lucky, the person you fancy got drunk enough to go home with you.
- Use the fact that you were so drunk to excuse any bad behaviour or the regrettable person you ended up waking up with the next day.

While these tactics can be quite effective, they are rather hit and miss and have some serious consequences. Most of the time you end up going home with someone you didn't really actively choose.

Student life is a crucial part of your flirting career, and many people meet their lifelong partner at university. College is your most important hunting ground for finding someone, and a great place to practise your flirting skills. It is also a very easy hunting ground. Everyone around you is generally the same age and you all have something in common – you are at university. In addition, almost everyone is single. This makes learning the basics of flirting at college more powerful. Many people mention how easy things seemed at university – well it is, so make use of it!

Working with the National Unions of Students in the UK, I developed a simple diagnosis tool for students, with study modules attached. The tool covered the areas where you can go right and wrong with flirting, and then specified modules for students to study flirting. What follows is an adapted version, with recommendations for chapters to study in this book.

Student flirting diagnosis

Questionnaire for men

Answer the following questions. At the end of the six questions, there is a list of chapters and sections that you can tick as you go through the questionnaire.

1 When you go to a party, do you pick out the top three people that you fancy?

☐ Yes – move on to question 2.

☐ No or sometimes – tick Chapter 3, 'Shopping problems' in the list, then move on to question 2.

2 Can you tell if a person fancies you and is giving you a green light signal and wants you to come and talk to them?

☐ Yes – move on to question 3.

☐ No or sometimes – tick Chapter 4, 'Men – spotting the green light' in the list, then move on to question 3.

3 Are you good at starting conversations?

☐ Yes – move on to question 4.

☐ No or sometimes – tick Chapter 5, 'Opening lines' in the list, and move on to question 4.

4 Can you tell if the person you are flirting with is interested in you?

☐ Yes – move on to question 5.

☐ No or sometimes – tick Chapter 7, 'Signs from women', in the list, then move on to question 5.

5 Does the person you are flirting with realize you are interested in them?

☐ Yes – move on to question 6.

☐ No or sometimes – tick Chapter 6 in the list and move on to question 6.

6 Do you get their phone number?

☐ Yes. Congratulations!

☐ No – tick Chapter 8 in the list.

Chapters or sections I need to re-read and master:

- Chapter 3 'Shopping problems' section ☐
- Chapter 4, 'Men – spotting the green light' section ☐

- Chapter 5, 'Opening lines' section ☐
- Chapter 7, 'Signs from women' section ☐
- Chapter 6 ☐
- Chapter 8 ☐

Questionnaire for women

Answer the following questions. At the end of the six questions, there is a list of chapters and sections that you can tick as you go through the questionnaire.

1 When you go to a party, do you pick out your top three people that you fancy?

☐ Yes – move on to question 2.

☐ No or sometimes – tick Chapter 3, 'Shopping problems' in the list overleaf, then move on to question 2.

2 Do the people that you fancy come and speak to you at bars and parties?

☐ Yes – move on to question 3.

☐ No or sometimes – tick Chapter 4, 'Women – giving the green light' in the list, then move on to question 3.

3 Do people you don't like often come and speak to you?

☐ Yes – tick Chapter 3, 'Signal failure in women' in the list, then move on to question 4.

☐ No or sometimes – move on to question 4.

4 Do the people you flirt with know that you fancy them?

☐ Yes – move on to question 5.

☐ No or sometimes – tick Chapter 6, then move on to question 5.

5 Can you tell if the person you are flirting with fancies you?

☐ Yes – move on to question 6.

☐ No or sometimes – tick Chapter 7, 'Signs from men' then move on to question 6

6 Does the person you fancy ask for your phone number?

' ☐ Yes – Congratulations!

☐ No or sometimes – tick Chapter 8 in the list.

Chapters or sections I need to re-read and master:

- Chapter 3, 'Shopping problems' section ☐
- Chapter 4, 'Women – giving the green light' section ☐
- Chapter 3, 'Signal failure in women' section ☐
- Chapter 6 ☐
- Chapter 7 'Signs from men' section ☐
- Chapter 8 ☐

If you master all of the chapters and sections you ticked in the questionnaire, you will find flirting as a student easy. Remember to make use of your time as a student – college is probably the best flirting hunting ground you will ever have!

Flirting for friends

When you first arrive at university, it can be an intimidating place. You may have left most of your friends behind and you need to start again from scratch. As well as getting you dates, flirting can also help you to make friends quickly and easily.

Step into their shoes

To be comfortable with flirting for friends, you should realize that everyone is in the same boat as you. They are all a little nervous and they are all keen to make new friends. Once you see this, feel this and talk to yourself about it, you will find making friends much easier.

I am now going to get you to step into another person's shoes. Once you actually feel, see and hear what it is like for them and understand how they see you, you will make friends more easily.

We are going to look and talk about your situation from your perspective, from the perspective of the person you are breaking the ice with, and from an outsider's perspective. You need three chairs, or enough space to sit in order to move around to three different spots. Position the chairs as shown in Figure 8.

Exercise

First position – me

Stand or sit in first position. Imagine you are breaking the ice with someone new at college.

Observer
Third position

<table>
<tr><td>

Me
First position

</td><td>

Potential friend
Second position

</td></tr>
</table>

figure 8 first, second and third positions

Right now, write down how it looks, sounds and feels to be you, and what you are thinking.

....

....

Second position – potential friend

Now stand up, have a stretch, and move to second position. Pretend you are stepping into a potential friend's shoes. Imagine where they are from, what course they are doing, and what it's like for them to be at college for the first time.

Right now, write down your thoughts here.

....

....

Look back at first position and see yourself standing there. Listen to yourself using the icebreaking lines and starting a conversation. Feel what it's like.

Right now, imagine you are the potential friend, write down how it looks, sounds and feels to have the person in first position start a conversation. Are you happy that they broke the ice?

....

....

Third position – observer

Now stand up, have a stretch, and move to the third position – the observer. Step into the observer's shoes. As the observer, imagine you are looking at and listening to the conversation between yourself and the potential friend. What does it look like, sound like and what is the observer thinking? **Right now**, write this down.

....

....

Final observations

Have a stretch and step back into first position. Look at the potential friend. What does the situation look like now? How does it feel now? What are you saying to yourself in your head? **Right now**, write this down.

....

....

Hopefully you have now experienced, seen and heard that the person you are starting the conversation with is in exactly the same boat as you. They are probably actually relieved that someone is making the effort to start a conversation! And, from the observer's perspective, it seems like a perfectly normal conversation between two new people at college. These new realizations will make it easier for you to break the ice.

Breaking the ice for students

Now that you have more of a sense that everyone is in the same boat, it's time to work on breaking the ice. Everyone is feeling shy, everyone is feeling confused, and lots of people are probably feeling excited. If you don't take the first step to break the ice, then you are leaving it to luck for friends to find you.

You are in a prime ground for flirting and making friends. Why? You all have something in common. You are starting something new and you are all in it together. This is the perfect starting point for making friends.

So, what sort of opening lines can you use to get a conversation started? The obvious ones are the best.

Weather comment

Take something in your local environment, or something that is happening to you both, and make a comment about it to the person you want to start a conversation with.

- 'This queue is slow!'
- 'This tour is really boring.'
- 'How long does it take to get served here?'

Information

Because you are all new and you don't know your way around, asking for information is another perfect way to break the ice.

- 'Do you know where X building is?'
- 'Do you know where I sign up for X?'
- 'Do you know where I go for X lecture/tutorial?'

Follow-up

You need to follow-up these opening lines with some other quick open questions. These are questions that require more than a yes or no answer, for example:

- 'So what do you think of freshers' week so far?'
- 'How's your first day (week) been?'
- 'What do you think of the lectures/tutorials so far?'

This is enough to break the ice and get the conversation moving. Next you need to listen to the person you are talking to and make them feel important.

Stay in touch – close the deal

As you have started the conversation and been doing the listening, it's your job to close the deal. If you think you'd like to hang out with the other person more, you have to take the initiative. When the conversation is drawing to an end, you can keep in touch comfortably by trying the following three-step process:

Stage 1 – Go over good stuff

Run over the good parts of the conversation again. Thank the other person for the information they gave, have another laugh about the jokes they told, repeat the things you have in common.

Stage 2 – Suggest a next time

Suggest something you could do together – meet up for a beer, go to a freshers' event together, catch lunch later. If they say yes, it means you've started making a new friend!

If they make some sort of excuse, or don't suggest anything else, just leave it there.

Stage 3 – make it specific and get their phone number

Make it specific – work out the time and place for meeting up again. Make sure you both know where it is. Swap phone numbers. Things can go wrong and plans change, so you need to be able to get in touch. Now it is simply a matter of meeting up and taking things from there.

Congratulations, you now have everything you need to start making new friends at university.

In summary:

- Step into their shoes – everyone at college is in the same boat as you; they will be happy if someone starts a conversation with them.
- Use icebreakers – weather comments or asking for information.
- Listening to someone with complete focus will make it much easier to make friends with them.
- Close the deal – suggest something else you can do together and arrange a specific time and place.

15

flirting in later years

In this chapter you will learn:

- how flirting in later years can be a challenge and what to do about it.
- how it can feel like a time machine has taken you to a strange new flirting future
- how 'shopping' is especially crucial.

In your later years, flirting can be more complex and difficult – especially compared to the easy flirting ground of college! As part of the older generation, you are probably more traditional. While the younger generation are much more fluid in their approach to flirting (many women are more willing to take a leading role), the older generation stick to the traditional flirting rules.

If you are part of this older generation, the basic rules of flirting are even more important. Women will expect the men to make the first move, and men will expect to take the lead role. At many events, older men are better at flirting than the younger generation. They recognize the signals, and are willing to take a strong leading role.

If you are a woman, it is vital that you understand that it is your role to choose the men you want to flirt with. Many of the older generation think that they want the man to make the first move, and are almost unwilling to give eye contact. However, it has always been the women who do the choosing. The men then take action and start the conversation . Make sure that you have mastered Chapter 5 on the basic rules of flirting.

Battle scars

When flirting, you may find that many of the people that you flirt with will bear battle scars. They have often been in long relationships, which tend to leave deeper wounds. You will need to be more gentle and patient with the people you flirt with. In addition, if you have been in a relationship for a very long period of time, particularly ten years or more, you may have turned off your flirting signals. This is a natural reaction to being in a relationship – why would you want to flirt with anyone else if you are already taken? The side-effect is that it can be even more challenging to turn your signals on if you come out of a long relationship.

This all means that learning and putting the basics of flirting into practice is even more important in your later years. Get it right, and you will have a big advantage over most other people in your age group!

You might like to re-read the section in Chapter 4 on ex-itis. If you have come out of a long-term relationship, you might be suffering from quite a severe case of ex-itis.

Tardis syndrome

If you have recently finished a relationship, you may also be suffering from 'tardis syndrome'. This is where you feel like you have stepped into a time machine and been thrown into a strange future where there is a dazzling array of technological ways to date, and all the rules seem to have changed.

Remember that although there are differences, the fundamentals are the same. In the past, you may have met a partner at a dance, or through friends, but now it is a matter of shopping in different places, but using the same basic rules.

Shopping is crucial

When flirting, finding the right places to shop for people is very important. Generally, single people over 50 find that all their friends are in relationships, which shuts off an important place to shop: among your friends' networks.

Make use of all the options that the modern dating world has to offer. Go along to dating events for your age group. They may be hard to find at first, but it is worth the effort. Dating events used to focus on the younger end of the market, but more and more companies are now looking at older target markets.

Get online – try internet dating. If you use popular websites, you will be pleasantly surprised at the number of people in your age bracket that you find. If you struggle with using the computers or internet, get some training. The internet could be your best chance of finding a new partner, and not using the internet could hold you back.

In summary:

- The basic rules of flirting are even more important in later years.
- People you flirt with may have battle scars, so be gentle and patient.
- It may feel like you have stepped into a time machine, but remember the fundamental rules are still the same.
- The internet can be particularly important if you are over 50 – it will widen your flirting opportunities!

16

conclusion

Congratulations. You have now taken your first step on what will be an exciting and rewarding journey in the world of flirting. You have the basic tools, the rules and the ways to overcome the major obstacles that might stand in your way. As when learning every new skill, there will be challenges – but the challenges will help you to hone your skills. You have the tools to take the pain out of any bumps you might hit, and this will give you the extra push to keep going.

By doing the exercises in this book, you have started to re-programme your mind for flirting success. Now you have to go out and put your new skills into action. Like learning to drive a car, it is getting out on the road that really counts. So, good luck with your flirting journey, I wish you well. It can be a lot of fun and open many doors. I hope it takes you to the place you want to reach.

If you have success stories, I would love to hear from you. **Email me at teachyourself@samvanrood.com.**

Good luck on your flirting journey!

taking it further

Further reading

There are many flirting books on the market. The ones below are a selection of the best material I have found. Tracey Cox is the undisputed queen of flirting, hence she features heavily in this list. I have also included some books on related topics such as confidence and NLP (neuro-linguistic programming).

Superflirt, Tracey Cox, Dorling Kindersley, 2003

Superdate, Tracey Cox, Dorling Kindersley, 2005

Hot Relationships, Tracey Cox, Corgi Adult, 2000

The SIRC Guide to Flirting, Kate Fox,
www.sirc.org/publik/flirt.pdf

How to Mend your Broken Heart, Paul McKenna and
   Hugh Willbourn, Bantam Press, 2003

Instant Confidence, Paul McKenna, Bantam Press, 2006

NLP Workbook, Joseph O'Conner, Cygnus Books, 2001

As well as coaching for flirting, I work with single people to find the relationship they want.

If you would like to find out more, or work with me personally, log onto my website www.samvanrood.com or email me at teachyourself@samvanrood.com

index

teach® yourself

From Advanced Sudoku to Zulu, you'll find everything you need in the **teach yourself** range, in books, on CD and on DVD.

Visit **www.teachyourself.co.uk** for more details.

Advanced Sudoku and Kakuro
Afrikaans
Alexander Technique
Algebra
Ancient Greek
Applied Psychology
Arabic
Aromatherapy
Art History
Astrology
Astronomy
AutoCAD 2004
AutoCAD 2007
Ayurveda
Baby Massage and Yoga
Baby Signing
Baby Sleep
Bach Flower Remedies
Backgammon
Ballroom Dancing
Basic Accounting
Basic Computer Skills
Basic Mathematics
Beauty
Beekeeping
Beginner's Arabic Script
Beginner's Chinese Script
Beginner's Dutch

Beginner's French
Beginner's German
Beginner's Greek
Beginner's Greek Script
Beginner's Hindi
Beginner's Italian
Beginner's Japanese
Beginner's Japanese Script
Beginner's Latin
Beginner's Mandarin Chinese
Beginner's Portuguese
Beginner's Russian
Beginner's Russian Script
Beginner's Spanish
Beginner's Turkish
Beginner's Urdu Script
Bengali
Better Bridge
Better Chess
Better Driving
Better Handwriting
Biblical Hebrew
Biology
Birdwatching
Blogging
Body Language
Book Keeping
Brazilian Portuguese

Gaelic
Gardening
Genetics
Geology
German
German Conversation
German Grammar
German Phrasebook
German Verbs
German Vocabulary
Globalization
Go
Golf
Good Study Skills
Great Sex
Greek
Greek Conversation
Greek Phrasebook
Growing Your Business
Guitar
Gulf Arabic
Hand Reflexology
Hausa
Herbal Medicine
Hieroglyphics
Hindi
Hindi Conversation
Hinduism
History of Ireland, The
Home PC Maintenance and
  Networking
How to DJ
How to Run a Marathon
How to Win at Casino Games
How to Win at Horse Racing
How to Win at Online Gambling
How to Win at Poker
How to Write a Blockbuster
Human Anatomy & Physiology
Hungarian
Icelandic
Improve Your French
Improve Your German
Improve Your Italian
Improve Your Spanish
Improving Your Employability

Indian Head Massage
Indonesian
Instant French
Instant German
Instant Greek
Instant Italian
Instant Japanese
Instant Portuguese
Instant Russian
Instant Spanish
Internet, The
Irish
Irish Conversation
Irish Grammar
Islam
Italian
Italian Conversation
Italian Grammar
Italian Phrasebook
Italian Starter Kit
Italian Verbs
Italian Vocabulary
Japanese
Japanese Conversation
Java
JavaScript
Jazz
Jewellery Making
Judaism
Jung
Kama Sutra, The
Keeping Aquarium Fish
Keeping Pigs
Keeping Poultry
Keeping a Rabbit
Knitting
Korean
Latin
Latin American Spanish
Latin Dictionary
Latin Grammar
Latvian
Letter Writing Skills
Life at 50: For Men
Life at 50: For Women
Life Coaching

Linguistics
LINUX
Lithuanian
Magic
Mahjong
Malay
Managing Stress
Managing Your Own Career
Mandarin Chinese
Mandarin Chinese Conversation
Marketing
Marx
Massage
Mathematics
Meditation
Middle East Since 1945, The
Modern China
Modern Hebrew
Modern Persian
Mosaics
Music Theory
Mussolini's Italy
Nazi Germany
Negotiating
Nepali
New Testament Greek
NLP
Norwegian
Norwegian Conversation
Old English
One-Day French
One-Day French – the DVD
One-Day German
One-Day Greek
One-Day Italian
One-Day Portuguese
One-Day Spanish
One-Day Spanish – the DVD
Origami
Owning a Cat
Owning a Horse
Panjabi
PC Networking for Small
  Businesses
Personal Safety and Self
  Defence

Philosophy
Philosophy of Mind
Philosophy of Religion
Photography
Photoshop
PHP with MySQL
Physics
Piano
Pilates
Planning Your Wedding
Polish
Polish Conversation
Politics
Portuguese
Portuguese Conversation
Portuguese Grammar
Portuguese Phrasebook
Postmodernism
Pottery
PowerPoint 2003
PR
Project Management
Psychology
Quick Fix French Grammar
Quick Fix German Grammar
Quick Fix Italian Grammar
Quick Fix Spanish Grammar
Quick Fix: Access 2002
Quick Fix: Excel 2000
Quick Fix: Excel 2002
Quick Fix: HTML
Quick Fix: Windows XP
Quick Fix: Word
Quilting
Recruitment
Reflexology
Reiki
Relaxation
Retaining Staff
Romanian
Running Your Own Business
Russian
Russian Conversation
Russian Grammar
Sage Line 50
Sanskrit

Screenwriting
Second World War, The
Serbian
Setting Up a Small Business
Shorthand Pitman 2000
Sikhism
Singing
Slovene
Small Business Accounting
Small Business Health Check
Songwriting
Spanish
Spanish Conversation
Spanish Dictionary
Spanish Grammar
Spanish Phrasebook
Spanish Starter Kit
Spanish Verbs
Spanish Vocabulary
Speaking On Special Occasions
Speed Reading
Stalin's Russia
Stand Up Comedy
Statistics
Stop Smoking
Sudoku
Swahili
Swahili Dictionary
Swedish
Swedish Conversation
Tagalog
Tai Chi
Tantric Sex
Tap Dancing
Teaching English as a Foreign
  Language
Teams & Team Working
Thai
Theatre
Time Management
Tracing Your Family History
Training
Travel Writing
Trigonometry
Turkish

Turkish Conversation
Twentieth Century USA
Typing
Ukrainian
Understanding Tax for Small
  Businesses
Understanding Terrorism
Urdu
Vietnamese
Visual Basic
Volcanoes
Watercolour Painting
Weight Control through Diet &
  Exercise
Welsh
Welsh Dictionary
Welsh Grammar
Wills & Probate
Windows XP
Wine Tasting
Winning at Job Interviews
Word 2003
World Cultures: China
World Cultures: England
World Cultures: Germany
World Cultures: Italy
World Cultures: Japan
World Cultures: Portugal
World Cultures: Russia
World Cultures: Spain
World Cultures: Wales
World Faiths
Writing Crime Fiction
Writing for Children
Writing for Magazines
Writing a Novel
Writing Poetry
Xhosa
Yiddish
Yoga
Zen
Zulu